SHIFTING SANDS

Andy Stoddart

HARRY — OUR WONDERFUL
NORFOLK — WHERE BETTER....

Ruth
x.

Other books by Andy Stoddart

The Birds of Blakeney Point
Prairie Dreams: *A Human and Natural History of North America's Great Plains*

SHIFTING SANDS

BLAKENEY POINT AND THE ENVIRONMENTAL IMAGINATION

ANDY STODDART

This image of a medieval 'cog' ship was used on early publications from Blakeney Point.

Copyright © Andy Stoddart 2013. All rights reserved. No part of this publication may be reproduced, stored in a retrieval system or transmitted, in any form or by any means, electronic, mechanical, photocopying, recording or otherwise, without prior permission of the author.

ISBN: 978-1484043011

Printed in the United States of America

Cover illustration: Aerial view of Blakeney Point (*Mike Page*)

To Maja

When we look at nature...we are looking mainly at ourselves.

Frank Stewart

Frontispiece. The Lifeboat House (*Andy Stoddart*)

CONTENTS

Prologue: The Nature of Imagination	1
1. What's Hit is History	5
2. Sea Swallows	21
3. Nature's Economy	39
4. Nature in Trust	57
5. Shifting Ground	79
6. Down the Long Wind	99
7. Seal Sands	121
8. Mindscape	135
Bibliography	151
Index	161

LIST OF PLATES

1. Bluethroat in the Suaeda bushes — 6
2. E.C. Arnold — 6
3. Sandwich Terns — 22
4. Bob Pinchen — 22
5. The Laboratory and the Tamarisk — 40
6. Francis Oliver with UCL students — 40
7. The Laboratory and the Plantation — 58
8. Arthur Tansley — 58
9. Aerial view of Blakeney Point — 80
10. Young dunes on the outer beach — 80
11. The 1961 Radde's Warbler — 100
12. Richard Richardson at the Hood — 100
13. Grey Seals on the outer beach — 122
14. A Common Seal cull — 122
15. The Watch House — 136
16. View across the Harbour — 136

ACKNOWLEDGEMENTS

I would like to thank all those with whom I have shared so many good times on Blakeney Point, most notably fellow birdwatchers Giles Dunmore, Pete Feekes, Steve Joyner, Tony Marr, James McCallum, Richard Porter, Chris Wheeler and Norman Williams and National Trust Wardens Joe Reed, David Wood and Eddie Stubbings and Assistants Aaron Boughtflower, Joe Cockram, Stefan McElwee, Jason Moss, Paul Nichols and Ajay Tegala.

Tony Leech, James McCallum and Richard Porter were all generous with their support and feedback on a draft version and Tony Leech also helped with image processing and technical issues.

I am also very grateful to Pam Peake and the Blakeney Area Historical Society for access to the Society's archive and to Norfolk Library Service for arranging the loan of reference material.

Thanks are also due to Julian Bhalerao, Mike Page, Richard Porter, Moss Taylor and the National Trust for the use of photographs.

Extracts from *Home Country* by Richard Mabey, published by Little Toller Books © Richard Mabey 1973 are reproduced by permission of Sheil Land Associates Ltd.

An extract from *The Eagle has Landed* by Jack Higgins (Michael Joseph, 2005), copyright © Jack Higgins 1975, 1983 is reproduced by permission of Penguin Books Ltd.

Finally, my thanks go to Maja Passchier for sharing long shingle walks and for her constant support.

Prologue

THE NATURE OF IMAGINATION

Every generation writes its own description of the natural order, which generally reveals as much about human society and its changing concerns as it does about nature.

Donald Worster

On East Anglia's northern coast, the gently rolling agricultural hinterland with its great rectangular fields, meagre hedges and scattered copses merges finally with the North Sea in a complex and shifting succession of grazing marsh, dyke, reedbed, saltmarsh, estuary mud and sand. At the outermost edge of this mosaic, where the sky is highest and where the eye finally scans a flat, far horizon, a long dune-capped ridge of shingle extends westwards and outwards into the sea, barely rising above it. This is Blakeney Point.

This is a place defined by its wildness, famous for its unique topography and flora, for its seals, its breeding terns and its migrant birds. At all seasons, it is a place of ever-changing moods, constantly reinvented by light, wind and tide. It is the 'jewel in the crown' of a remarkable stretch of coast.

But there is more to Blakeney Point than landscape quality and wildlife. Here can be found a fascinating human as well as natural history, a story of wildfowlers, collectors, protectionists, ecologists, conservation planners, geographers, ornithologists, birdwatchers, seal tourists, fishermen, artists and writers. This is a story not of landscape transformation, the familiar theme of most environmental history, but one of ideas, of what we have known and imagined about nature, and of how, like its sands, these understandings and perceptions have always shifted.

In the closing years of the nineteenth century Blakeney Point was the prime destination for the Victorian bird collector. Its Suaeda bushes provided a host of new and important bird discoveries but also a revealing insight into contemporary society, its social and economic preoccupations and its attitudes towards wild creatures. Soon, however, such pursuits were overtaken by the wholly new notion that birds and other animals might be worthy of protection rather than persecution. As these ideas developed, Blakeney Point remained centre-stage, hosting the country's earliest experiments with practical species protection regimes.

At the beginning of the twentieth century the study of botany was transformed into a new discipline known as 'ecology' and, by chance, Blakeney Point became the outdoor laboratory and intellectual home for its leading figures. The study of its plant communities contributed greatly to our knowledge but also to the wider international debates over the direction and role of this new science. The 'Blakeney Point ecologists' were also instrumental in protecting the Point as Britain's first coastal nature reserve and later went on to frame the ideas behind the planning of Britain's post-war network of statutory scientific reserves.

Meanwhile, the north Norfolk coast had been discovered by coastal geographers, Blakeney Point providing the classic case study in the development of shingle spits, dunes and saltmarshes. This work created the new science of coastal geomorphology but it also challenged our traditional notions of landscape permanence, an understanding underlined dramatically by the infamous 'storm surge' of 1953. At the same time the Point found itself part of the expanding bird observatory movement. Its studies of migration yielded a wealth of important facts but, just as importantly, they tapped into an age-old fascination and inspired a whole new generation of birdwatchers with an enthusiasm which persists to this day.

Today, in a new century, Blakeney Point is still somewhere to think about our place in nature. This shingle ridge has always been synonymous with seals, and its seal-watching trips are famous, but our relationship with these animals has a long, complex and contradictory history. The Point therefore poses difficult questions about our relationship with these, and indeed all, wild creatures. Blakeney Point also asks us about our relationship with landscape. Long regarded as remote, marginal and unappealing, it has today been transformed into a 'designer destination'. A hundred years after its acquisition for essentially scientific reasons, the Point teaches us that we value places not according to how they really are but according to how they are perceived.

Blakeney Point has always found itself at the forefront of new knowledge and new ideas. It has reflected our understandings and our perceptions of nature, holding up a mirror to how we view the natural world, but it has also been a pioneer, inspiring us to extend what we know and to explore new ways of seeing and thinking. Today Blakeney Point remains an intellectual testing ground, a laboratory of the imagination. It asks us not only what we know about nature but also how we think of it, how we value it and how we might best be part of it.

Blakeney Point is therefore a place of cultural as well as environmental importance. There is, however, no written record of this unique contribution. The bibliography of Blakeney Point, the repository of our knowledge of this remarkable place, is extensive but it is written almost exclusively in the language of science, fragmented, compartmentalised, more concerned with facts than with ideas. This book attempts to fill this gap. It sets out to document Blakeney Point's role in uncovering new knowledge and nurturing new thinking but it also explores the often deep historical contexts to these ideas, tracing the connections between the story of this shingle ridge and the shifting sands of our environmental imagination.

Andy Stoddart
April 2013

1

WHAT'S HIT IS HISTORY

What's hit is history, what's missed is mystery.

Henry Seebohm

In the closing years of the nineteenth century Blakeney Point was discovered as a haunt of Bluethroats and other rare migrant birds. It quickly became the prime destination for the Victorian bird collector and this previously obscure shingle ridge was propelled to national fame. Its Suaeda bushes went on provide a host of new and important bird discoveries which filled the journals and museum cabinets of a new generation of amateur scientists. However, the Victorian collecting craze was about more than science. Concerned as much with outdoor recreation, competition and financial advantage as with scientific discovery, it reflected contemporary society, its wider social and economic preoccupations and, perhaps most of all, its attitude towards wild creatures.

Plate 1. Bluethroat in the Suaeda bushes (*Richard Porter*)

Plate 2. E.C. Arnold

It is 12th September 1884 and the sky is lowering and grey. There is rain in the air and a chill east wind is gusting and shifting restlessly into the north. Two men plod slowly and systematically through Blakeney Point's crunching shingle, pressing with difficulty through the tough and brittle Suaeda clumps. Suddenly, a small dark bird darts out almost from underfoot and flies ahead fast and low, hard to follow against the dark background. At first glimpse it resembles a Robin but it is perhaps a darker, more steely grey-brown and as it lands it fans its tail momentarily to reveal unexpected flashes of bright orange. The men's pace quickens. The bird is flushed once more but this time it loops back, attempting to pass behind. A shotgun is raised, its barrel catches up with the bird's trajectory, there is a dull 'crack' and the bird falls to the shingle. Almost stumbling, the men run to claim their prize. Turning it over they see a whitish stripe over its eye, prominent dark marks at its throat sides and, across its breast, bands of orange and the purest sky blue. It is a Bluethroat.

In 1884 this was considered to be one of the rarest as well as the most beautiful and most desired birds on the British List. Breeding in mountainside willow and birch scrub in Scandinavia, the Bluethroat's normal migration route to winter quarters in Africa should take it well to the east of Britain. Its first British appearance had been as recently as 1826, in Newcastle, its only previous occurrence in Norfolk being a bird found dead on Great Yarmouth beach in 1841.

These two men, Fred and George Power, had visited the area in the hope of rare waders but, in their tramp through the bushes and dunes, they had made an unexpected but much more significant discovery. Nor were their excitements over. As the day progressed, these London doctors went on to record not just one Bluethroat (though that would have been reward enough) but a veritable avalanche of the species, at least eighty, perhaps even a hundred! They also recorded a host of other migrant birds. Only days before, on 4th September, they had shot Norfolk's first and Britain's third Barred Warbler, a large grey warbler from the thickets of eastern Europe. Blakeney Point's secret had finally been unlocked.

The Power brothers went on to write up their experiences in 'Ornithological Notes at Cley and Blakeney, September 3rd to 19th 1884', published in the *Transactions of the Norfolk and Norwich Naturalists' Society*. Of 12th September they write that 'the day was passed at the sandhills, and a most prolific haunt they proved. Bluethroats were present in extraordinary numbers, for we reckoned those seen at from eighty to one hundred'. They go on to describe the 'Blue-throated Warbler' as the commonest small migrant recorded during their visit.

As a result of these revelations, Cley saw a sudden influx of visitors keen to add to their collections not only a Bluethroat but perhaps even a bird new to the British List. Though collectors were already seeking migrant birds at a number of other locations - in Yorkshire and Lincolnshire, in east Norfolk and in Kent and Sussex - the discovery of Bluethroats on Blakeney Point propelled this largely unknown and unvisited shingle spit to a position of instant fame and celebrity. The new visitors were to transform the fortunes of Cley and the neighbouring villages.

By the closing years of the nineteenth century, the heyday of the Glaven ports already lay far in the past. The slow and inexorable westward growth of Blakeney Point, the silting of the increasingly-confined estuary, the building of reclamation banks and the trend to ever larger ships had long ago snuffed out their lucrative international trade. The area was now a rural backwater, its population no longer making a living from commerce but from more traditional pursuits, from a shifting mix of farming, fishing, shellfish and samphire gathering, wildfowling and shore-shooting.

The local wildfowlers worked the whole stretch of coast from Salthouse Broad to East Hills, Wells and they knew the area intimately. They knew, for example, that the Cley Channel was amongst the most reliable spots for flighting ducks and that the Stiffkey outflow never froze, even in the harshest conditions. The toll on birds from these activities was considerable. A contemporary account notes that in 1889 a punt-gunner in the estuary fired three shots, the first killing 120 Knot, the second eight Shelduck and the third twenty-seven Brent Geese. The account also notes that:

> In the early morning [of 17th February 1901], just as day was breaking, Geo. Long and his son and T. Cringle of Wells with their gun punts drew up to a flock of Knot, computed at between four and five thousand. They fired simultaneously at about 80 yards distance and the result was 603 Knot, 9 Redshank and 6 Dunlin. It took them till 10.30 to collect the dead and wounded.

This was a challenging and often dangerous pursuit, however, initially carried out with long-barrelled muzzle-loaders fired from the shoulder or from a punt. The wildfowler ran the constant risk of injury from an exploding weapon, and a number of local men suffered badly from such mishaps.

The area had been popular with visitors since at least the 1860s but these early gunners were after wildfowl and waders. Sporadic shooting at ducks would take place from 1st August but the season for waders began on 1st September. Then, as many as forty gunners might be out on the estuary. A contemporary account notes that:

> A party of gentlemen from Norwich, who generally put in an appearance the night before the 1st so as to be on the estuary by daybreak, got as usual a large bag, 156 of all sorts and ages, from full-grown tern to birds that could scarcely rise from the ground. I

was told by a gentleman who went to the Point on 3rd and 4th that he did not see a Common Tern at all during the two days.

The shooting was clearly indiscriminate, encompassing not just wildfowl and waders but also Blakeney Point's breeding terns and their chicks, indeed any birds which happened to present themselves were fair game. Particularly popular were the Pallas's Sandgrouse. This normally very rare Central Asian species is prone to very occasional westward irruptions which may bring it to Britain. Such was the case in 1888, with a considerable flock favouring a field between Blakeney and Morston, and many were shot, both here and on Blakeney Point.

It was, however, the Power brothers' discovery of Bluethroats and other rare small migrants which was to have the most lasting impact. Here was a whole new draw and a whole new business opportunity. The visitors required a wide range of services including lodgings and food, the use of boats and the expertise of local wildfowlers, gunners and taxidermists. This new trade was to transform the local economy, bringing a welcome seasonal 'boom', and in August and September the talk was of little besides the pursuit of rare birds. Soon it became easier to get here too. In 1887 the Midland and Great Northern Railway came to Holt, from where Cley and the ornithological riches of Blakeney Point were but a short pony trap ride away.

These collectors, or 'gentlemen gunners' (for they were exclusively men), were products of the new Victorian craze for collecting. The study of nature was by now a well-established, legitimate and respectable activity. With increasing propsperity and leisure time, the middle and upper classes had begun to seek healthy and morally uplifting pursuits. Providing both mental and physical stimulation, the study of natural history was ideal, and the leisured class had begun to invade the countryside in ever-increasing numbers. Here, roaming the fields and woods, they could combine healthy exertions with educational self-improvement.

Few possessed any formal scientific training and fewer still were professional scientists but, with sufficient time and money, anyone could found their own collection and acquire the status of an 'expert'. Fossils and shells, beetles and butterflies, ferns and flowers and, increasingly, birds and mammals were all pursued with enthusiasm and displayed with pride.

A number of developments had come together to enable this social transformation to take place. First, the incorporation in 1758 of binomial nomenclature into the tenth edition of Carl Linnaeus's *Systema Naturae* provided a wholly new framework within which the natural world could be categorised. Previously there had been no discernible order to the study of natural history. Species had been named arbitrarily according to their physical characteristics and confusion had reigned. In this new order all living creatures were given a binomial, a two-part name, conferring both a genus and a species. These in turn fell within a broader system of families, orders, classes and phyla. Suddenly, order had replaced chaos.

This new vision was to inspire other ideas and approaches. New 'scientific' disciplines were adopted. Specimens were observed, collected, described and classified. If they were deemed 'new to science' they were accorded the status of a 'type specimen', their 'type locality' was recorded and their existence was published in a scientific journal. The further study of geographical variation led to the concept of the 'subspecies', recognised through a new trinomial nomenclature. However, Linnaeus's system provided more than the foundation for a new scientific profession. Its neat categorisation of nature also presented species as a set of commodities, as things which could be collected.

Technological developments also fuelled this new interest in nature and the countryside. The printing press brought books within reach of more people and increasing levels of literacy meant that more people could read them. Gilbert White's now celebrated *The Natural History of Selborne*, largely ignored since its publication in 1789, suddenly acquired a new and eager readership. The quality of book illustrations also improved, expensive and laborious woodcut and metal plate engraving replaced by lithography. Important texts for the aspiring ornithologist soon emerged, notably the American Elliott Coues's 1890 *Handbook of Field and General Ornithology*, a veritable treasure trove of advice and encouragement for the collector. Birds 'should be sought everywhere, at all times', advises Coues. 'How many birds of the same kind do you want?', he asks before answering the question himself: 'All you can get'.

Other inventions also aided the would-be naturalist. The microscope transformed the study of plants and insects whilst the Wardian glass case enabled specimens to be displayed to one's peers in attractive settings, poses and compositions. The development of breech-loading double-barrelled shotguns and fine shot cartridges meant that it was now possible to shoot small birds without obliterating them entirely and new taxidermy techniques meant more durable and visually attractive specimens.

Meanwhile, improving transport and communications had led to increased mobility and a new appetite for travel. Key advances were more rapid and reliable mail services and better roads, but the most important development was the coming of the railway. Those with sufficient money could now escape the cities and travel the length and breadth of Britain in search of specimens.

Better communications led in turn to increased contact between enthusiasts and a proliferation of clubs and societies to organise and direct this new quest for knowledge and specimens. The Linnaean Society was formed in 1791, the Zoological Society of London in 1826 and the Entomological Society in 1833. These were followed by the British Association for the Advancement of Science, the Botanical Society of London, the British Ornithologists' Union and a host of others. Most published journals to report on the rapidly increasing body of knowledge in their field. *The Zoologist* was first published in 1843 and *Ibis*, journal of the British Ornithologists' Union, first appeared in 1859. With the expansion of Britain's empire, such pursuits were also exported around the world and great collections were assembled by a new generation of intrepid explorers and collectors such as Howard Saunders, Alfred Wallace and Henry Seebohm.

At Cley, the most prominent of the collector naturalists was E.C. Arnold, a teacher at (and ultimately the headmaster of) Eastbourne College. His final book *Memories of Cley*, published in 1947, provides perhaps the best and most complete account of the heyday of collecting in the area and includes his own bird notes spanning the years 1896 to 1928.

Arnold lists those who first collected birds here: the Connops (father and son), Reverend E.H. Ashworth and, of course, the Power brothers. He writes of the latter's 'discovery' of Blakeney Point in his typically strained poetry:

> Thee did the Powers by intelligent scrutiny
> mark on the map as the place for a prize;
> sought thee for waders and found in astonishment
> warblers fresh in from Siberia's skies.

Arnold's Cley contemporaries represented the next generation, amongst them Colonel W.A. Payn (reputedly the 'most scientific' of the collectors), T.E. Gunn of Norwich (famous for having downed an Aquatic Warbler and a Great Snipe with left and right barrels in the Sandhills), Frank Richards (a London solicitor who never missed a season before the First War) and Clifford Borrer (who was to settle in Cley at the Old Manor House). Arnold also mentions a number of other less regular visitors, referred to somewhat disparagingly as 'quasi-collectors'.

The local gunners and the gentlemen collectors represented, of course, opposite ends of the social spectrum and there was inevitably some friction between them but nevertheless mutually beneficial business arrangements soon developed. The collectors employed the services of a number of local men to act as beaters and to find, and sometimes shoot, the best birds for them. The Power brothers had hired William Brent, otherwise known as

'Old Bloke', but in Arnold's day the most sought-after for this work were 'Old Bishop', M.A. Catling and, above all, Ted Ramm and Bob Pinchen (and their dogs 'Duchess' and 'Prince'). Frank Richards would offer employment for ten shillings a day and would also offer the same amount for any new bird which they were able to add to his collection. Richards often used to stay on *Britannia*, a fishing boat beached near the tip of the Point. Here he was right amongst the birds, downing them even from its decks. The young Billy Bishop of Cley, whose father assisted Richards, recalls carrying beer and cartridges to *Britannia* for two shillings a week and bringing back unwanted waders to be made into pies.

Whenever a wind from the east promised an arrival, the collectors would descend on the bushes full of anticipation. As a finder of rare birds, Arnold rated Ramm the most highly:

> He was a great authority on the weather as it affected bird migration, keeping a constant eye on the charts and always hoping for a "through wind", and though good birds did sometimes turn up, when he didn't expect them, yet when he prophesied that they would be there the prudent made tracks for the bushes at once.

The techniques deployed were systematic and ruthless, Borrer reporting that:

> Every sort of device was tried to induce the birds to show themselves, including the dragging of chains and ropes through the bushes. But the only effective method was the use of a suitable dog... what was neded was a close-ranging animal which would move from side to side in front of the guns, causing the birds to flutter forward above the shrubs or to fly out on the flanks affording the wing-gunners a clear shot.

Arnold participated in these activities with great enthusiasm. His diary entry for 5th September 1902 notes that the bushes held:

... one warbler, darker and greener, as I thought, than a Chiffchaff. It seemed to possess a charmed life, for I pursued it till my barrels were red hot and my No. 8 cartridges gave out. I was then reduced to shooting at it with a No. 4, after which it soared wildly up with hanging legs and finally dropped in thick bush, where I was never able to find it!

By now breech-loading guns had replaced muzzle-loaders. As well as being safer, these offered more shots per minute and could be fired into the air. 'Shoot first and check later' seems to have been the prevailing philosophy and stories abound of buckets of Robins and Redstarts discarded in the quest for rarer quarry.

For all the collectors the Bluethroat remained the iconic bird, the 'signature species' of Blakeney Point, and the one which they most wanted to acquire. It took Borrer a long time to secure one and so great was his joy on finally doing so that he duly threw up his hat and fired his second barrel through it. Arnold commemorated the event:

Here did a hunter in joyous abandonment
Loose of his gun and dismember his hat,
When the slim Bluethroat, so often his conqueror,
This time triumphant he put on the mat.

Borrer also recounted his own success, remembering:

... the eagerness with which I followed up every chance of securing an Arctic bluethroat, until one stormy September morning I had the thrill of bagging a beautiful cockbird with a sky-blue gorget.

Arnold lavished particular praise on this species, claiming that 'the combination of beauty and rarity is unusual and irresistible'. He placed it (albeit with a little exaggeration) 'in the Roller class'. The most desirable of all were the occasional adult males which still sported a satin blue breast. In the hands of the right taxidermist these would make the most pleasing specimens and attract the greatest envy and admiration.

At the centre of this new industry was Henry Nash Pashley of Cley, latterly Ted Ramm's father-in-law. In 1884, the year the Power brothers discovered the Point's Bluethroats, he became a full-time professional taxidermist. He was clearly skilled in the art, winning a prize in a bird-stuffing competition with a flying Turnstone. Pashley's workshop soon became an essential gathering place for collectors, gunners and dealers alike, Arnold noting that:

> ... he was a splendid natural host and his stuffing room was a sort of naturalists' club, to which every shooter brought his rarities, even if he was going to stuff them himself; in fact a visit to Pashley's was a bird education in itself.

Pashley died in 1925 but the same year saw the posthumous publication of his *Notes on the Birds of Cley*, a collection of bird observations from Cley and Blakeney Point between 1888 and 1924. In its Foreword, the Norfolk ornithologist Bernard Riviere remembers Pashley with fondness:

> ... the hours passed all too quickly whilst one listened to his tales of bird-life on this bleak North Norfolk coast. Outside, when at last one left, was the smell of the sea and the call of migrating birds passing overhead, and the memory of that small, enchanted room, with all its associations, will live long in one's pleasantest dreams.

The writings of both Arnold and Pashley reveal a near-constant procession of rare and valuable birds. In 1890 there was a diminutive Red-breasted Flycatcher from the woods of eastern Europe and, in 1894, a tiny, striped Yellow-browed Warbler from the birch forests of northern Siberia, amongst the first ever recorded in Britain. Pashley notes of this latter occurrence:

> The first Yellow-browed Warbler for Norfolk was taken on this date. This bird was shot with a 10-bore gun and very large shot. Its head

was nearly severed and the rump and intestines almost entirely shot away so the sex could not be determined. The man who shot it fired off his battered old muzzle loader at the first bird he saw rather than take it home loaded.

Further Yellow-browed Warblers were recorded at Blakeney Point in 1907, 1908 (when three were seen) and 1910 but in 1896 Ted Ramm shot perhaps the greatest prize of all, an even more tiny, and even more beautiful, Pallas's Warbler from southern Siberia, the first ever to be found in Britain and known in Europe only from two occurrences on the German island of Heligoland. Of this exciting discovery the noted ornithologist Henry Dresser recounts the following:

> One of the most interesting additions that has of late been made to the avifauna of the British Islands is certainly that of Pallas's Willow Warbler (*Phylloscopus proregulus*), a single example of which was shot at Cley-next-the-Sea, Norfolk, on the 31st October 1896 by Mr. Ramm.... he "found it amongst the long grass on the bank or sea-wall, not far from the sea at Cley, a locality which has produced many rare migrants, and at first took it for a Goldcrest, but on aproaching to within two or three yards, the bird being very tame, he thought he recognised a Yellow-browed Warbler, a species he had seen before, and therefore secured it".

This famous bird was subsequently sold to Ernest Connop for the sum of forty pounds and passed into his collection at Rollesby Hall before being sold to W.R. Lysaght of Chepstow. He in turn donated it to the City of Birmingham Museum where it still resides.

Other rare birds were soon to follow, including Norfolk's first Icterine Warbler (from the woods of central Europe) in 1899, secured by Arnold himself. The new century saw further rarities from Russia, Arnold shooting Britain's first Yellow-breasted Bunting at the Watch House on 21st September 1905. His notes in *Memories of Cley* recount the event:

Near the Watch House Streeten and I started a bird which we took at first for a very yellow Meadow Pipit. After several misses I at length shot it and then grasped that it was a small bunting. Its flight was of the pipit type rather than that of a bunting. Everyone in the village declared that this was a young Yellowhammer except Pashley, who, on a second visit after I had stuffed it, wound up thus: "Well, sir, I believe you've got a good one".

But it was not only Pashley that Arnold had to convince. He also had to persuade the ornithological establishment of the day that he had secured something special. An article by Percy Trett in the *Eastern Daily Press* in March 2005, drawing on a conversation with John Gledhill and the journals of his grandfather, provides a fascinating insight into its workings:

One September morning, the late E.C. Arnold, the scholar naturalist, shot a small bird perched on the roof of the old Pilot House on Blakeney Point. He knew it was a bunting, but he did not recognise the species. So, that evening he skinned his prize and preserved it for when he next attended a meeting of the British Ornithologists' Union at Paganini's restaurant in London where, for the sum of 7s 6d, eminent ornithologists could sit down to an excellent dinner and could exhibit their trophies over coffee and cigars. In due course Arnold's little corpse was produced and deposited on a clean plate and a waiter summoned to take it to the chairman for inspection. John's grandfather was present and recorded that he observed a somewhat puzzled expression come over the bearded countenance of Lord Rothschild, who was presiding.

Again and again he picked it up and laid it down. He ordered another bottle of Paganini's best wine and the bird was handed around the learned gentlemen on the top table. Many a wise head was bent over it and a smile appeared on Arnold's face as Gledhill senior remarked "You have stumped Rothschild!" Dr. Ernst Hartert, the curator of Tring Museum, was called. Hartert leaned across and whispered something into Rothschild's ear. He nodded, gavelled the august meeting to silence then, holding up the specimen as though he had recognised it at first glance, announced "Mr. Arnold is to be congratulated on adding a new species to the British List. His bird is undoubtedly a Yellow-breasted Bunting".

Other Blakeney Point rarities from those years include a Desert Wheatear from Central Asia in 1907, a Little Bunting from Scandinavia in 1908, another Yellow-breasted Bunting in 1913 (also obtained by Arnold) and, on 4th September 1922, England's first Arctic Warbler (then known as Eversmann's Warbler), also discovered and secured by Arnold. His diary takes up the story:

> After lunch Strong and Howell went off to Morston and I sat down on the beach to wait for their return. Fortunately I had a sudden fit of restlessness and went for a prowl along the edge of the marrams, nearest to the sea. Just as I reached the Cart Road, out flashed a "Yellow", which gave the impression of having a barred wing. Another view of it, as it flew towards the estuary, confirmed this idea and I shot it beside the track. I then saw that the bar, though faint and small, was obviously there, and it also had a marked eyestripe and mottled cheeks; in fact I realised that I had got a rare good bird, since it was bound to be either an Eversmann or a greenish Willow. I was in the collectors' seventh heaven once again.

Many of these birds are documented in an *Annotated List of the Birds of Blakeney Point, Norfolk*, published in 1918 by William Rowan, a student from University College London and regular visitor to the Point. Much of its content was gleaned from 'numerous pleasant chats' with Pinchen and Ramm and, as do the publications of Arnold and Pashley, it constitutes a fascinating historical record not only for the details of the birds documented in its pages but for the insights it provides into the world of the gunners.

At least some rationalised their pursuit of birds as a purely scientific enterprise, a quest for new knowledge and valuable museum specimens. Rowan, for example, notes that the use of a gun 'renders a great service to ornithological knowledge', and much of ornithological value was indeed learned from the efforts of the collectors. Their specimens often found their way into museum collections and their sightings into the new scientific journals. For many, however, the scientific motive was little more than a gloss. More powerful motivations were the pursuit of outdoor enjoyment, personal prestige and financial gain.

In reality, the quest for specimens occupied a distinctly blurred territory on the boundaries of science, leisure, country sports and commerce. This is seen most clearly in the strangely ambiguous language used to describe their activities. They were not scientists or ornithologists. Instead they were 'gentlemen collectors' or 'sportsman naturalists'. Collecting was, above all, great fun, an enjoyable leisure pursuit with all the characteristics of a sport. Competition was a key element of its appeal as enthusiasts and collectors strove to make their mark by acquiring the largest and most complete collections or, better still, by discovering a new species. Inevitably, specimens acquired financial as well as scientific value and a whole economy of taxidermists and dealers grew up to make money from the collecting craze.

For most, collecting was a highly acquisitive, competitive occupation, as much a social and economic phenomenon as a scientific one, and, perhaps as a result, its heyday was brief. Public taste moved on and the cases of stuffed birds and other animals, once so popular, went out of fashion. In the end, the collecting craze proved to be little more than a passing fad, a product of a particular time and circumstances.

Its demise was also signalled by a slow change in public sensibilities. Away from the happy hunting grounds of Blakeney Point new ideas about our place in nature had been taking shape. In the minds of some, and particularly in the minds of some women, birds were not simply the object of dispassionate enquiry or the currency of personal ambition, there to be massacred at will. For some, wild creatures deserved not a blast from a shotgun but respect, compassion and concern.

2

SEA SWALLOWS

*Kill not the Moth nor Butterfly
For the Last Judgment draweth nigh.*

William Blake

The Victorian collecting craze was to be a temporary phenomenon. The idea that wild creatures existed purely to be killed had deep historical roots but it was nevertheless slowly overtaken by the new notion that birds and other animals might be worthy of protection rather than persecution. Such thoughts arose first in the minds of a few enlightened individuals, often women, and were pursued mainly through the passing of legislation but Blakeney Point was also to play a key role in developing these new ideas, hosting the country's earliest experiments with practical species protection regimes. These were hugely successful, leading to dramatic increases in the Point's breeding birds and providing a model for protection schemes everywhere.

Plate 3. Sandwich Terns (*Julian Bhalerao*)

Plate 4. Bob Pinchen

In spring Blakeney Point is transformed, not just by the sudden warmth in the sun nor by the growth and flowering of plants but by the arrival of a new presence. Just as the Swallow marks the coming of summer for most, here the turning of the year is confirmed by the arrival of the terns. The comparison goes further, however, for the terns are still frequently known by their traditional name of 'Sea Swallows'. Rakish, sharp-winged and streamer-tailed, they provide, on the coast's outermost fringe, a perfect counterpoint to the familiar Swallow of house and barn.

If the Bluethroat is (or at least used to be) the 'signature species' of autumn, the terns provide the characteristic sights and sounds of spring. The first to return is the Sandwich Tern, the largest, noisiest and most dramatic of Blakeney Point's terns. The frontrunners arrive from West Africa in the closing days of March, riding the first mild winds of spring, and soon many hundreds are gathering around the far spits. At such times their vigorous aerial displays are hard to miss. With loud and strident 'kirriks' pairs climb high into the sky until they are mere shining points of light. Finally they descend as if on a rollercoaster, swooping and swerving and filling the air with their calls. From now until their departure in September the 'kirrik' of Sandwich Terns is the quintessential sound of Blakeney Point.

During April the colony begins to settle and, as the month progresses, the Sandwich Terns are joined by others, Common and Little Terns, also from West Africa, and, from the Southern Oceans, a handful of Arctic Terns, perhaps the greatest bird travellers on earth.

The size and composition of the Blakeney Point tern colony has constantly changed. The traditional terns here were the Common and Little Terns. No-one knows when they began to nest but the presence of the former has been documented since at least 1830. Sandwich Terns, by contrast, were almost unknown until the closing years of the nineteenth century and did not begin to breed in any numbers until the 1920s. Today this is the dominant tern species, with over 3,000 pairs in some years, almost a quarter of the British breeding population. This is now Blakeney Point's most important breeding bird species.

Such success has not come about by accident, however. Today the Point is watched over by a team of dedicated Wardens whose primary task is to protect the colony. The threats are many: disturbance from humans and dogs, egg collectors, weather and tides and, most significant, a long list of predators, from Rats, Stoats and Foxes to gulls, Kestrels and even Short-eared Owls. These threats are mitigated by a range of tried and tested measures such as excluding dogs in the breeding season, fencing off and watching over the breeding areas, providing information to the public, either directly or through signage, and trapping mammal predators.

The need for such measures is today widely recognised and supported but little more than a century ago wildlife protection was a barely-understood concept. The prevailing attitude towards wild creatures was entirely practical. They were there to be eaten. At best, they were viewed with indifference. This view stemmed at least partly from traditional beliefs. Religious orthodoxy dictated that the world had been created for man alone and that other species were there purely to meet his needs. Man had been created superior to animals and he had God's permission to use them as he wished and without restraint. To the religiously-inclined there was a huge weight of theological justification available for this view. 'Every moving thing that liveth shall be meat for you', declared Genesis ix 2-3.

But there were also other factors besides religion driving our relentless assault on wildlife. Economic forces and the power of the market played their part, as did the new disciplines of science. For the prophets of the Enlightenment, the purpose of science was not to understand nature so as to protect it but to study it to see how it could best be used, to master it, manage it and exploit it ever more systematically and efficiently. Far from bringing us closer to nature, the early study of natural history was utilitarian, practical and exploitative in its motivations.

In this context there was, unsurprisingly, little or no consideration of the hunted animal and any sufferings it might endure. The natural world lay outside man's moral framework and most gave the feelings of animals little thought. Wildlife was slaughtered across the land, for food, for profit, for sport or purely for amusement. Across the British countryside, birds and other animals were pursued and abused through a seemingly endless list of 'country pursuits': trapping for the cagebird trade, bird-liming for the pot, egg-collecting, pheasant-shooting, grouse-shooting, wildfowling and duck-decoying, deer-hunting, hare-coursing, fox-hunting, otter-hunting, badger-baiting, cock-fighting and 'predator' and 'vermin' persecution, this latter category encompassing everything which competed for man's resources, from Sparrowhawks and Jays to House Sparrows and Bullfinches. Something of the scale of this activity can be deduced from contemporary accounts. Thomas Pennant, Gilbert White's correspondent, writes of 48,000 Skylarks being killed on the Dunstable Downs in a five-month period whilst 22,000 Wheatears were said to have been trapped each year on the South Downs above Eastbourne.

Prior to the advent of firearms in the seventeenth century the extent of the slaughter had been relatively modest but their invention revolutionised hunting and with the replacement of the muzzle-loaded shotgun by the breech-loader in the nineteenth century the massacre increased in both its scale and intensity. The list of bird extinctions is long and includes Avocets, Spoonbills, Great Bustards, Cranes, Ospreys, Goshawks, Marsh Harriers and White-tailed Eagles. For most, the first reaction on seeing a rare bird was to shoot it.

All sections of society, urban and rural, young and old, rich and poor, men and women, participated in this orgy of killing but different occupations were, of course, reserved for different social classes. The poor might trap small birds and shoot Rabbits and pigeons whilst the rich pursued 'nobler' quarry - deer, Pheasants and Red Grouse - on their estates, at the same time paying their gamekeepers to eliminate everything deemed a threat to their quarry.

Only a few animals found themselves exempt from this assault. Those most useful to man, such as dogs and horses, had long been prized for their utility and regarded with pride or even fondness. Slowly, however, such feelings began to be extended to other creatures. By the mid-eighteenth century came the first stirrings of unease over the way in which wild animals were being treated. A few began to argue that whilst it might be acceptable to kill wild creatures for economic reasons, for food or if they were harmful to man's interests, killing for pleasure and unnecessary cruelty should be avoided. Little by little, killing was becoming controversial.

The first real action was taken on behalf of farm animals and pets. Acts against cruelty to horses and cattle were passed in 1822, and in 1824 the Society for the Prevention of Cruelty to Animals was formed. Initially concerned with domestic animals, its remit was soon extended to include all wild creatures. Further legislation followed (in 1839 and 1854) to ban cruelty to dogs, and cock-fighting was outlawed in 1849. The first steps to including animals within both a moral and a legal framework had been taken.

Such progress was very much in keeping with the times. The Romantic movement of the late eighteenth and nineteenth centuries sought a new relationship with nature. Turning their backs on the new economic forces of the Industrial Revolution and on the cold detachment of science, the Romantics articulated an increasingly sentimental view of animals and birds. In particular, a new generation of poets began to speak out against animal cruelty. Coleridge's *Rime of the Ancient Mariner* can be seen as a morality tale constructed around the killing of the albatross whilst perhaps the most celebrated moral interjection is William Blake's *Auguries of Innocence*:

A Robin Redbreast in a Cage
Puts all Heaven in a Rage.
A dove house fill'd with doves and pigeons
Shudders Hell thro' all its regions.
A Dog starv'd at his Master's Gate
Predicts the ruin of the State.
A Horse misus'd upon the Road
Calls to Heaven for Human blood.
Each outcry of the hunted Hare
A fiber from the Brain does tear.

This new climate of opinion opened the way for other less artistic but more practical interventions. In 1868 the East Riding Association for the Protection of Sea Birds was formed in response to the annual slaughter of auks and Kittiwakes on the cliffs of Bempton and Flamborough, much of it to supply the newly-burgeoning fashion for wearing exotic feathers in ladies' hats.

Influential voices soon joined the cause, amongst them such early ornithological luminaries as Charles Waterton, Reverend Francis Morris and Alfred Newton, the latter Professor of Zoology at Cambridge and founder of the British Ornithologists' Union. The new interest in science and natural history had inspired in most a desire for specimens but, in the minds of a few, it had also spawned a wholly new idea, that of species protection.

1869 saw the successful passage through Parliament (supported by the RSPCA) of the Sea Birds Protection Act. Though justified partly on humanitarian grounds (gulls helped rid farmers' fields of pests and guided fishermen back home, it was argued), the Act introduced the new notion of a 'close season' for hunting, in this case from 1st April to 1st August, and it applied to thirty-three species, though precisely which were covered remained a little vague. The Act covered, for example, Guillemot, Razorbill and Puffin but also 'Auk', 'Murre' and 'Sea Parrot', Kittiwake but also 'Tarrock', Gannet but also 'Solan Goose' and, no doubt confusing for any visitor to Blakeney Point, both 'Sea Swallow' and 'Tern'. As well as being confusingly drafted, the Act was also far from comprehensive for the eggs of these species remained wholly unprotected. Egg-collecting therefore continued on a massive scale. At Bempton alone, some 130,000 Guillemot eggs were taken in 1884.

Further legislation followed, however, in the form of the 1872 Wild Birds Protection Act and the 1876 Wild Fowl Protection Act. In the latter, many duck species, including Teal and 'Widgeon', were protected in the breeding season, defined as lasting from 15th February to 10th July. The 1876 Wild Birds Protection Act extended the close season and increased the number of species protected whilst an 1880 Act introduced a close season of 1st March to 1st August for all birds.

Nevertheless, the millinery trade continued to grow. This was now a huge and lucrative business and, with the home supply unable to meet the demand, feathers from pheasants, birds of paradise, herons and egrets were increasingly sought in the furthest reaches of the Empire and shipped back to Britain.

Opposition continued to grow, however, and in 1876 Newton wrote a celebrated letter to *The Times* to protest at its excesses. Soon, more collective action was being organised and women began to take the lead. Inspired by such writings as Eliza Brightwren's *Wild Nature won by Kindness*, two groups of concerned women sprang up at opposite ends of the country: a Plumage League in Manchester and a Fur, Fin and Feather Group in Croydon. Eventually both organisations merged to form the Society for the Protection of Birds, a new base was established in London and what was soon to become the Royal Society for the Protection of Birds was born.

The appeal to the public was at first an emotional one, focusing on the impact of killing adult birds and leaving their young defenceless in the nest, but there were other triggers too. The

1888 irruption to Britain of Pallas's Sandgrouse from Central Asia led to a country-wide massacre of these rare and beautiful birds, including at Blakeney Point, but it also fuelled an outraged reaction in many and a call for more effective protection legislation. Concern for wild birds was also bolstered by the hard winter of 1890/91 which prompted a new habit of feeding the birds in the garden. In the wake of this experience, bird tables and nestboxes became suddenly popular.

The newly-formed Society for the Protection of Birds enjoyed the patronage of many prominent figures in society and the ornithological establishment including Lord Lilford, Sir Edward Grey and, of course, Newton. Perhaps most prominent, and certainly most articulate, was the naturalist and writer W.H. Hudson.

Hudson was brought up in Argentina where he had roamed the countryside in pursuit of birds and butterflies, snakes and spiders. After moving to Britain in 1874 he became a prolific author, the leading nature writer of his generation, publishing by the time of his death in 1922 over forty books on birds and natural history. Hudson became an influential figure in shaping contemporary attitudes to wildlife, particularly birds, both popularising them in the public mind and inspiring support for their protection.

It was, however, not science which motivated Hudson. Instead, he drew his inspiration from nature's beauty. His writings contain not just observations of birds but a deep and often sentimental appreciation and a sense of kinship and attachment to fellow creatures. In his 1913 *Adventures amongst Birds* he refers to the 'feathered people' who inspire in him 'a glorious gladness'. Part nature writing, part travleogue, this collection of essays expresses tenderness, emotion and a spiritual connection with birds of the kind normally reserved for people or pets. For Hudson, birds were not the objects of cold, dispassionate scientific study. They were his friends.

Such sentiments, very much in the Romantic tradition, are unfashionable today and Hudson is now little read but his writings chimed well with the changing attitudes of the late nineteenth century. Hudson was a vigorous opponent of hunting and an outspoken advocate of bird protection. In the very first chapter of *Adventures amongst Birds* he cautions the reader that, despite its title, he will find within its pages:

> ... no adventures of a wild-fowler... no thrilling records of long nights passed in a punt, and the glorious conclusion of the adventure when he happily succeeds in sending a thousand pellets of burning lead into an innumerable multitude of mallard, widgeon, teal, pochard, and pintail.

As well as books, Hudson wrote a number of letters and leaders in *The Times* and a series of leaflets on subjects such as the plumage and cage-bird trades. In one of these, entitled *Lost British Birds*, he notes:

> It is very difficult to determine which of the following three inveterate bird-destroyers have done, and are doing the most to alter, and, from the nature-lover's point of view, to degrade, the character of our bird population - The Cockney sportsman, who kills for killing's sake; the gamekeeper, who has set down the five-and-twenty most interesting indigenous species as 'vermin' to be extirpated; or, third and last, the greedy collector, whose methods are as discreditable as his action is injurious.

Hudson drew his ideas and inspirations from a host of locations but amongst his favourite places was the north Norfolk coast, particularly the great saltmarsh between Wells and Blakeney Point. Here, the pleasures he takes from birds are in stark contrast to those of the wildfowlers and gentlemen collectors.

One late autumn day he comes across a typical sight, a tired Redwing fresh in from the North Sea. This forms the catalyst for the essay *A Tired Traveller*. The tone of this piece is strongly anthropomorphic, somewhat jarring to modern sensibilities, but it illustrates Hudson's attempt to connect with the wild birds he encounters. Of the thrushes he notes that 'all of this family are dear to me' but the Redwing he considers to be 'I think, the most charming'. Brought to a state of rapture by his meeting and subsequent 'conversation' with this Redwing, he concludes his essay:

> It darkens my mind to think that man should invent and practise every conceivable form of persecution and cruelty on these loveliest of our fellow-beings, these which give greatest beauty and lustre to the world.

Modern authors have given Hudson's contribution rather mixed reviews. He was no scientist, and some have criticised him for his lack of detailed knowledge and scientific curiosity. He famously once declared (wrongly) that the St. Kilda Wren was extinct. But such criticisms miss the point. Hudson was nature's dramatist, not its analyst. He was a literary interpreter and advocate of the natural world, a master of the written word, and his influence on contemporary thought was profound.

Thanks to the efforts of Hudson and others the embryonic bird preservation movement gained much popular suppport. It secured further protection legislation through a succession of new Acts though egg-collecting remained entirely legal. Of course these developments represented considerable progress but the cause of conservation still had a long way to go. The young movement was firm in its belief that legislation (rather than education or habitat protection) was the best way to achieve its goals and, in its campaigns, the prime focus was always on birds.

It is not hard to understand the popular appeal of birds. They are widespread, attractive, often colourful and sometimes beautiful songsters but the public's concern for this group was inevitably at the expense of other creatures. Sentimentality went only so far. Birds were an easy campaign subject but other animals were much more troublesome. Could the public be equally motivated by the plight of Otters and Badgers and, if so, what about Foxes or, indeed, Rats? The early protectionists were, in effect, highly selective, pursuing not a holistic and inclusive vision of nature but a highly partial one.

Nor did this new movement represent a broad swathe of public opinion. Anxiety over the fate of birds was, in reality, limited to a narrow social group comprising the urban rich upper and middle classes and, at least initially, mainly women. Nor was there any great push for conservation from within the scientific community. The surprisingly rapid progress of protection legislation reflected not a groundswell of public opinion but rather the influential position of those involved in the campaign. Out in the countryside the rural poor carried on pretty much as they had before, as did the gentry on their estates and the gentlemen collectors wherever they scented a rarity.

The early bird protection legislation therefore ran well ahead of public attitudes and common practice and, unsurprisingly, it was, to start with, largely ineffective. To make matters worse, in many cases the drafting was less than clear and the loopholes were many. The new laws were, for a time, widely ignored, barely enforced and, even when they were, the financial penalties were minimal.

On Blakeney Point, as everywhere else, the early protection legislation made little practical difference and things carried on pretty much as they had always done. The terns were still shot every summer and their eggs collected, whilst wildfowling, punt-gunning, shore-shooting and specimen collecting were constant and indscriminate.

Things were eventually to change, however. Blakeney Point could not be isolated forever from the new world taking shape around it. The new protection legislation first made itself felt with the conviction of a local boy for the shooting of two Roseate Terns in June 1896. The fine and costs amounted to twenty-three shillings and sixpence but these were paid for him by Henry Pashley.

Much more organised intervention came in 1901 when, at the instigation of Quentin Gurney of Northrepps Hall, a number of concerned local individuals came together to form the Blakeney and Cley Wild Bird Protection Society. This was the third such group to be formed in Norfolk. The first had been established in

1888 at Breydon Water where a 'Watcher' had been employed to police the close season and bring prosecutions against any who disobeyed the law. Next had come a Protection Society for Wells, established by Charles Hammond of Twyford Hall. He and a number of friends had funded a Watcher for the Little Tern colony at Stiffkey.

The creation of these Protection Societies stemmed from the recognition by a handful of enlightened local people that legislation alone was insufficient and that, to bring about any effective protection, supplementary local action was required. This was a pioneering and visionary approach, the first instance of practical species protection in the country, and Blakeney Point was to be its most important test-bed.

The first step was to recruit a Watcher to look after the tern colony in the breeding season and, after due consideration, Bob Pinchen, local wildfowler and former assistant to the gentlemen gunners, was appointed to the task. In Pinchen's 1935 *Sea Swallows*: *Reminiscences of a Bird-Watcher on Blakeney Point*, he records the occasion:

> Charles Hammond of Twyford Hall first mooted the idea of a bird sanctuary. He spoke to me on the subject and asked if I would like to become the Watcher. There being other aspirants, however, a meeting was held at Cley at which I was appointed to act for ten weeks of each nesting season at the weekly wage of 15 Shillings.

This appointment was a very shrewd one. As a local man, and a wildfowler himself, Pinchen knew the Point, its surroundings and its local characters well. As 'poacher turned gamekeeper' he was admirably placed to mediate between competing interests. He also had a deep affection for the area, writing in *Sea Swallows* that 'Blakeney Point was to me and is a wonderful and fascinating place'.

At first he lived on *The Ark*, a converted lighter, before moving to *Chance*, a rented Lowestoft fishing lugger later renamed *Britannia*. Pinchen was to live on (and later own) *Britannia* for twenty years before finally moving into the Lifeboat House.

By this time both the Point and the Lifeboat House were owned by the National Trust and Pinchen had become a Trust employee. He was only employed in the breeding seasons until 1921 (retaining his old occupation as a butcher) but thereafter he became full-time. In *Sea Swallows* he recalls the occasion:

> I was offered a wholetime engagement but having at that time a wife and eight children dependent on me I had to refuse owing to the inadequacies of the remuneration. This, however, was increased to my satisfaction and I was duly installed in my work at Blakeney Point.

Pinchen noted that the Common Terns usually arrived on or around 26th April, with nesting underway by May 8th-10th. At this time, visitors to the Point were allowed to wander around the tern colony but Pinchen took to marshalling their movements, 'stick-marking' the nests to avoid the well-camouflaged eggs being trampled and also keeping a look out for egg collectors. Under this new regime the breeding birds, not just the terns, flourished. Previously absent due to persecution, Oystercatchers returned to the Point to breed in 1906 and Common Terns increased from 140 pairs at the beginning of the century to 600 pairs by 1914 and a staggering 2,000 pairs by 1923. Little Terns were up to 100 pairs by 1912 and, from 1922, even Arctic Terns began to breed, albeit in small numbers.

Perhaps most dramatic of all was the arrival of the Sandwich Tern. Previously an almost unknown bird along the coast, a few started breeding in 1920 and there were 300 pairs by 1924. This had increased to 1,000 pairs by 1928 and 1,500 pairs the following year. By this time Black-headed Gulls, once a threatened species, were also breeding.

Given this level of success it was inevitable that there would be antagonism towards the terns from local fishermen who, in Pinchen's words, 'complained of the havoc created by their voracity' and claimed that 'they destroyed the young flat fish'. The number of flatfish began to decline in the 1920s for the simple reason, argued the fishermen, that Pinchen was protecting too many terns. As a consequence the Ministry of Fisheries gave permission for a small number to be 'obtained' and for them to be sent to the Yorkshire Museum for stomach anlysis. This task was duly performed by Pinchen in 1925 and forty-eight Common Terns, nine Sandwich Terns and six Little Terns were shot and sent off for examination. Not a single flatfish was found, however, and the terns breathed a little more easily thereafter. In subsequent years the fishermen began to take out visitors by boat to see the tern colony.

There was also much antagonism between the growing ranks of the protectionists and the gentlemen gunners. A letter by H.J. Massingham to the *Eastern Daily Press* in 1928 complains bitterly that:

> As soon as the close season ends, the beaches, dunes, saltings, the very sea are invaded by predatory parties of gentlemen-gunners who turn the whole place into something like a shambles.

Massingham's letter distinguishes between the two categories of gunner:

> The first is the so-called shore-shooter, who spends a congenial holiday in annoying and outraging every other visitor to this beautiful place by potting at anything he can get near enough.

The second category, the collector:

> ... prowls at the edge of the saltings and among the suaeda bushes to destroy the weary migrant on the chance that some of the victims may be rarities.

The letter closes with a plea for the National Trust to take some action. Following its acquisition of the Point in 1912, the Trust had continued to permit shooting but nevertheless the gunners found their activities increasingly curtailed. Eventually, the shooting would be outlawed altogether but in the meantime the gunners were not about to give up their fun without a fight.

Each side was, of course, firmly entrenched in its views. The protectionists accused the gunners of excessive killing, citing instances of buckets of Robins and Redstarts discarded in pursuit of a Bluethroat, whilst the gunners rejected such stories as wild exaggerations and inventions. For their part, the local wildfowlers felt that they, rather than the gentlemen gunners, were being disproportionately accused of misdemeanours by the protectionists. There was a lighter side to the arguments, however. E.C. Arnold describes how Colonel Payn once shocked the residents of the Blakeney Hotel by claiming that he would be devoting his whole week to shooting Goldcrests for a pie.

Arnold has much to say on these controversies in *Memories of Cley*. 'Farewell to thee, Cley, ere these fool laws constrained thee', he laments. Referring fondly to the 'good old days' before protection, he argues that collecting has considerable scientific value in its contribution to museum collections and that the bush-shooting is 'the least harmful that could be devised'. In a fit of exasperation with the contemporary 'protection mania', 'protection fanatics' and 'mad protectionists' he complains that:

> In Norfolk, so lost to all sense of proportion are the natives, that it is cheaper for the lethally minded to murder half a dozen children with a motor car than to kill one protected bird with a gun.

The student William Rowan took a similar view:

> Numerous sentimentalists object to this practice at any time of the year. The compiler of this list must differ from them, and on the following grounds. I do not suppose that a single one of the Blakeney Point breeding birds ever remains through the Autumn and Winter, so that shooting during the legitimate season can scarcely affect these. Moreover, all those numerous records of rarities that the Point can claim are isolated examples of birds that come either from the north of Continental Europe or from America, birds that never have and never will nest in our own country, and the shooting of these can affect neither our native bird population nor that of the localities from which these individuals hail.

Despite all the protestations and counter-arguments, however, Arnold and his fellow gunners were really the threatened species. The steady ratcheting up of the protection legislation in the early years of the new century led to the slow but inevitable extinction of the gentlemen collectors and to ever greater restrictions on wildfowling.

By 1931, the year of Pinchen's retirement, much had changed. Pashley, soured by the whole protection issue, had died in 1925 and the collectors were gone. Pinchen was now spending his time not just on protecting the tern colony but in developing a new educational role, speaking and lecturing to schools and other visitors. By the time he retired the basic management philosophy and practices for Blakeney Point were in place and continue little changed to this day.

By now the pioneering Norfolk Wild Birds Protection Societies had become increasingly formalised and a consolidated Wild Birds Protection Committee had been set up in 1921 to oversee protection schemes across the county. The new ideas developed and implemented at Blakeney Point had also become a model for species protection regimes elsewhere. The RSPB employed its first Watcher in 1901 to protect breeding Pintails at Loch Leven in Fife and by the time of the First War this was an important area of its work.

Pinchen's long stewardship of Blakeney Point's birds saw him transformed from wildfowler and gunners' assistant to active conservationist. His tenure also marked a turning point in attitudes, a transition to a new and more enlightened relationship with wild creatures. Today the spirit of these pioneering days lives on. Pinchen's beloved spaniel 'Prince' lies in the Plantation where, on long summer days, the loud 'kirrik' of Sandwich Terns still sounds out above the dunes.

3

NATURE'S ECONOMY

Ecology... is not only a fascinating study in itself but a subject with many practical bearings because it lies at the foundation of all the industries which depend on the management and use of vegetation.

Arthur Tansley

At the beginning of the twentieth century botany was transformed into a new discipline known as 'ecology', the study of shifting plant communities replacing traditional taxonomic approaches. By chance, Blakeney Point became the outdoor laboratory and intellectual home for the leading figures of this new science. The study of the Point's mobile vegetation systems contributed greatly to our knowledge but also to the wider international debates over the direction and role of ecology. Blakeney Point's ecologists had a utilitarian vision for their science, regarding it as the means to exploit natural resources for economic ends. They faced, however, an intellectual challenge from an equally deep-rooted but more biocentric and arcadian tradition, one which saw the natural world not as something to be managed and exploited but as something which demanded a more ethical and respectful engagement.

Plate 5. The Laboratory and the Tamarisk (*Andy Stoddart*)

Plate 6. Francis Oliver (right) with UCL students

Every year Blakeney Point sees a transformation. In winter it is a sombre place of muted hues, the shingle an unremitting grey, relieved only by the pale stalks of Yellow Horned-poppy and the darkly funereal Suaeda bushes. But each year brings a reinvention and the Point becomes splashed with, in turn, the delicate pink and white of Thrift and Sea Campion, the paintbox yellow of Yellow Horned-poppy and Sea Aster, the shimmering purple haze of Common Sea-lavender and the red and orange of Samphire.

Perhaps surprisingly, Blakeney Point is botanically rich. The bare shingle might look dry and barren but this is an illusion. In reality, the pebbles are highly effective at trapping rain and dew. Much organic material is also washed in and, in some parts, this is supplemented by excrement and dead birds from the breeding colony. This allows a succession of plants to take hold. Yellow Horned-poppy is an early colonist but others quickly follow: Common Ragwort, Curled Dock, Sea Campion, Sea Sandwort and Biting Stonecrop. Along its southern fringe, where the shingle meets the upper border of the saltmarsh, lies the belt of Suaeda, or Shrubby Sea-blite, bushes, a woody shrub highly tolerant of saltwater immersion and burial by mobile shingle. A Mediterranean plant, it is here at one of its most northerly locations. Nearby, above the reach of all but the very highest tides, the ground on the lateral ridges is more stable. Here a soil covering has developed and with it a rich sward of grasses.

Towards the Point's western end lies its second major habitat, the dunes. These demonstrate a complete range of stages of development, from tiny accumulations of wind-rippled sand and the first growth of Sand Couch and Marram Grass to tall, mature dunes with such characteristic plants as Grey Hair-grass and Sand Sedge. Mosses and lichens develop too and the sand turns from its young yellow colour to a striking grey. Other plants such as Bramble, Elder and Rose-bay Willowherb may grow on the dune sides.

The final major habitat is the saltmarsh. At first Eelgrass takes hold on the sloppy mud but as the mud dries it is colonised by Samphire. Then comes Sea Aster and, as creeks form, Sea-purslane spreads out from their edges until eventually a complex community of plants grows up to create a mature saltmarsh. Over time this rises higher and higher against the inland side of the shingle, constricting the tide to narrower and ever more sinuous channels. A wide variety of micro-habitats now exists, the lower reaches inundated twice-daily, the higher parts only a few times each year.

Today it has become the convention to talk of such plant communities, of vegetational succession, of plants, and indeed the rest of the natural world, as a great complex web of evolving relationships. The study of these processes is now universally understood through the term 'ecology'. The word was first used in 1866 by the German scientist Ernst Haeckel, defining 'oecologie' as 'the science of the relations of living organisms to the external world'. Haeckel had coined a new word for a new branch of science but it was not a wholly new idea.

The Linnaean legacy ensured an early focus on the description of individual species and their variation but by the nineteenth century science slowly began to acquire a new, more holistic and more connected vision of the natural world. Species of plants and animals, some realised, did not exist in isolation. They were part of a wider and more complex natural system. What was truly important was not the names of things but the relationships between them. Traditional taxonomy was slowly becoming ecology.

This new understanding of the natural world was perhaps most explicit in the work of the German explorer-naturalist Alexander von Humboldt. Humboldt had studied a host of disciplines including geography, geology, botany and climatology and developed the notion that plants formed discrete communities in accordance with the prevailing climatic conditions. In 1807 he published in his *Essay on the Geography of Plants* a new geographical approach to botany, grouping plants according to habitat.

These new ideas were soon taken forward both in Europe and in the New World. After Haeckel's coining of the term 'oecologie', others began to flesh out the boundaries of this new science and, by the end of the nineteenth century, ecology was beginning to acquire a more recognisably modern form.

In 1895 came yet another defining text, the Danish botanist Eugenius Warming's *Plantesamfund*, later translated into English as *The Oecology of Plants*: *An Introduction to the Study of Plant Communities*. This was the first botanical text to move beyond traditional floristic description and articulate a new type of study into the interactions between plants and their environment or, as Warming put it, 'the manifold and complex relations subsisting between the plants and animals that form one community'. Increasingly the talk was of assemblages or societies of plants rather than systematics and classification. Plant species were no longer viewed as isolated entities to be studied out of their natural context, as was the fashion of taxonomic botanists. Instead they formed part of a wider ecological community.

Much of this new thinking came from America. Inspired by Warming's work, Henry Chandler Cowles studied vegetational succession in Indiana whilst, on Nebraska's rapidly-advancing settlement frontier, Frederic Clements rushed to record the native flora before it was ploughed into oblivion. Clements went on to publish in 1916 his most important work, *Plant Succession*: *An Analysis of the Development of Vegetation,* its influential conclusion being that vegetation is an essentially dynamic 'community', constantly evolving, renewing itself after any 'disruption' and moving through a predictable sequential process which he termed 'succession' towards a single mature stage adapted to the prevailing climate. This he called the 'climax condition'.

Though initially a botanical science, Clements's collaborations helped ecology to move away from its traditional focus towards a more integrated vision which embraced terrestrial fauna and aquatic communities as well as flora. New terms were needed for these concepts, and 'bioecology', 'biotic community', 'biome' and 'biota' entered the lexicon.

In Britain such ideas were also taken up by a new generation of home-grown ecologists. They pursued their studies at a variety of locations at home and abroad but, almost by accident, the most important site in the early development of British ecology was to become Blakeney Point.

The Point's great botanical interest had long been noted. The Cambridge botanist Charles Babington had visited as early as 1834, collecting plants and noting in his journal that 'we went upon the bank of shingle that divides the marshes and the harbour from the open sea. Walked as far as the Blakeney Meals'.

It was, however, a botanist from University College London who was to secure Blakeney Point's lasting contribution. His name was Francis Wall Oliver. Following trips to Germany in 1885 and 1886, during which he associated with the country's leading plant geographers, Oliver developed a keen interest in ecology and in 1888, at the age of twenty-four, became Head of the UCL Botany Department. By 1890 he had followed in his father's footsteps and become its Quain Professor.

Oliver's early scientific pursuits were focused on palaeobotany but he soon became most interested in studying the vegetation of maritime habitats, undertaking a number of field trips to the Channel Islands and to northern France. Between 1904 and 1907 he made a particular study of the saltmarshes and dunes of Brittany's Bouche d'Erquy, the results of which were published in *New Phytologist.*

Visiting Blakeney for the first time in 1908, in order to recuperate from a bout of pleurisy, he was quick to recognise the area's scientific potential, in particular the further opportunity to study mobile vegetation systems rather than traditional static botany. Blakeney Point, he soon realised, was a botanist's dream, the perfect natural laboratory. Its relentless westward growth and constant reshaping by the sea meant that a complete range of successional stages was visible in one place. Here could be studied the slow succession of vegetation to a state of relative stability as well as the consequences of sudden and dramatic 'disruptions'. The Point, noted Oliver with enthusiasm, revealed 'the operations of Nature in its most dynamic form' and he swiftly transferred his attentions to this exciting new study site.

Oliver gained rapid agreement to establish a field station on the Point, and the old Lifeboat House was purchased in 1910 for the sum of fifty pounds. This marked the beginning of a long and productive relationship between UCL and Blakeney Point, and Oliver took students here for at least a fortnight every summer until he retired in 1929. He also made many other visits, either with colleagues or advanced students. In 1913 a purpose-built laboratory was constructed further back in the dunes and the Point became, in Oliver's words, 'the theatre of systematic studies at the hands of organised parties'.

Oliver was clearly enthralled with his discovery of Blakeney Point and conspired to spend as much time there as possible, noting wryly that 'the immediate problem... which confronts the ecologist attached to a seat of learning is how to make good his escape from his urban laboratory for the six summer months'.

All this activity was to result in a wealth of published work by Oliver, his colleagues and his students, much of which appeared in *New Phytologist*, *Journal of Ecology* or the *Transactions of the Norfolk and Norwich Naturalists' Society*. Most notable was a series of twenty-nine 'Blakeney Point Publications' covering subjects as varied as topography, vegetation (including pioneering aerial surveys), the tern colony and the food of Rabbits.

Amongst the most important is Oliver's 1912 paper in *New Phytologist* on 'The shingle beach as a plant habitat', the first classification of different types of shingle beach and the first attempt to link these types to the vegetation they each support. In 1913 he published 'Some remarks on Blakeney Point, Norfolk' in the first issue of *Journal of Ecology*, publishing in the same journal in the same year 'Vegetation on mobile ground as illustrated by *Suaeda fruticosa* on shingle', a collaboration with another prominent UCL botanist and ecologist (and later to be Oliver's successor as Quain Professor of Botany) Edward James Salisbury.

Also in 1913, another collaboration with Salisbury - 'Blakeney Point, Norfolk: Topography and Vegetation' - was published in *Transactions*. Oliver's introductory paragraph to this work sets the scene:

> The object of the present paper is to present an epitome of the salient facts of the constitution and distribution of the plant populations of the well-defined area of maritime waste lands known as Blakeney Point.

Oliver's use of the term 'waste lands' is highly revealing. For its author, ecology was an unashamedly utilitarian discipline with clear economic motives. The purpose of ecology (or, as he calls it, 'economic botany') was not to feel closer to nature but to understand its workings and thereby assist in the exploitation of its resources. These ideas are most clearly expressed in his 1917 edited work *The Exploitation of Plants* in which, in his Editor's Introduction, he argues that 'wild plants are exploited much less than might be expected. Their exploitation requires fertility in ideas and courage in their development'. Calling for a great national effort, he proposes that 'the whole empire should march together in this matter of the development of its resources'.

In his own chapter, entitled 'Waste Lands', Oliver uses the term to designate those areas not currently put to productive use. He argues that a small proportion of the country's 'waste land', perhaps a quarter, should be retained as a 'reservation' but the remainder, the vast majority, should be devoted urgently to economic use.

Amongst those habitats requiring such treatment are dunes, shingle beaches and saltmarshes. He argues that sand dunes should be afforested with conifers, as at nearby Holkham, that the Marram Grass should be harvested for paper production and that bulbs and vegetables should be grown commercially. Trees should be planted on shingle beaches to consolidate their role as sea defences while mudflats and saltmarshes should be reclaimed for agriculture. Here he proposes the planting of *Spartina townsendii*, an invasive hybrid grass, for the purposes of cattle feeding and paper manufacture.

These ideas provide the necessary context for understanding Oliver's interest in Blakeney Point and the purpose of his research activities. He was particularly interested in the experimental introduction of non-native plants and in differential plot management so as to understand which plants might best be suited to the native conditions. The legacy of these experiments is still evident today in the small plantation of Corsican Pines and White Poplars, the Tamarisk by the Laboratory, the large Yucca on the side of the dunes and the now extensive *Spartina* marsh.

Oliver retired from UCL in 1929 and took up a post at the Egyptian University, Cairo the following year. Here he continued with his studies of vegetational succession, now in a desert context, and was lauded by his new students as the 'Mohammed of Botany'. He left this institution in 1935 to live thirty miles west of Alexandria at Burg-el-Arab, remaining here even when closely approached by Rommel's forces in 1942. Oliver returned to England in 1950 and died the following year.

Oliver's greatest legacy is widely considered to be his pioneering work in the study of vegetation as a dynamic system. In developing this line of study he saved British ecology, in the view of his obituarist Edward Salisbury, from remaining mired in static taxonomic botany.

However, Oliver's most significant contribution to ecology was perhaps not his own research at all but his influence over the career of a young student and protégé named Arthur George Tansley, destined to become Britain's most influential and most-lauded ecologist of the early twentieth century. Whilst still at Cambridge Tansley attended classes held at UCL by Oliver and from 1893 to 1906 he was Oliver's assistant, helping him with his studies of coastal vegetation and working to establish the university as the leading centre of botanical study and teaching. Tansley was, like Oliver, greatly influenced by the work of Warming, Cowles and Clements and shared the new ecological philosophy:

> When the vast majority of species of flowering plants at least have been described, our attention must be more and more turned towards acquiring a knowledge of the associations or combinations in which plants occur.

In 1902 Tansley founded and edited a new journal, the *New Phytologist*, publishing only two years later 'The Problem of Ecology', regarded as British ecology's founding paper. The same year saw the establishment of a Committee for the Survey and Study of British Vegetation, with Tansley as its first Chairman. Through this committee Tansley drew up a set of rules for the classification and mapping of vegetation types and in 1911 produced *Types of British Vegetation*, a visual presentation of Britain's botanical landscape. In the same year he was to organise the first International Phytogeographical Excursion, a 'grand tour' around Britain to encourage collaboration between the leading botanical lights of Britain, Europe and America (including, from the latter continent, Frederic Clements). On 6th August, under the guidance of Oliver, this group travelled to Blakeney Point where they were able to examine its vegetational successions at first hand.

Tansley's already successful career soon went from strength to strength. In 1913 came the formation of the British Ecological Society, with Tansley installed as its first President, and he soon became Editor of its new *Journal of Ecology*, the very first issue of which contained Oliver's paper on Blakeney Point. Tansley himself published widely, both studies of particular locations and their plant communities and more wide-ranging pieces on the history, definition and future direction of ecology. In 1924 he was appointed Chairman of the British Empire Vegetation Committee and in 1939 came one of his most important publications, *The British Islands and their Vegetation*, in which the work undertaken by Oliver and others at Blakeney Point features prominently.

Such detail is perhaps necessary as it demonstrates Tansley's importance as the 'father of British ecology' but it also illustrates the pivotal role played by Oliver and their Blakeney Point experience in shaping his ideas. These influences moulded Tansley's view of what ecology was and what it might contribute to science and society, a vision which was to become the accepted, 'official' line, at least in Britain, for half a century.

However, Tansley was not to have complete control over the soul of ecology. This was still an evolving science and there were other perspectives too on what ecology might mean and to what use it might be put. Nowhere is this more clearly highlighted than in Tansley's professional clashings with one of his Blakeney Point companions of 6th August 1911: Frederic Clements of Nebraska.

Tansley was most troubled by Clements's notion of plant 'communities' and the implication that plants might be engaged in some grand cooperative enterprise, acting as a kind of 'complex organism'. He argued that vegetation may appear to show some of the characteristics of an organism, perhaps even a 'quasi-organism', but Clements's analogy went too far; vegetation was ultimately a collection of individual organisms. In place of 'community', Tansley coined the now dominant term 'ecosystem' in an attempt to employ more 'neutral' language and to cleanse ecology of what he regarded as dangerous 'subjectivity'. This quest for scientific rigour, what he himself termed 'the disinterested pursuit of knowledge', would become a recurring theme in his writings.

But the clash between Tansley and Clements was much more than an academic argument over semantics. More troubling, at least for Tansley, was Clements's notion of a single climax condition and the fundamental questions which this posed about man's place in nature. The American's position was that while natural forces (weather, ice ages, animal grazing, even native peoples) contributed to the creation of a natural climax, modern man did not. His manipulation of the environment was, argued Clements, a 'disruptive' force of a different scale and nature entirely.

For Clements, the natural climax presented a ready 'yardstick' against which man's environmental disruption could be measured. Implicit in this was a negative assumption against human impact, in particular that of modern intensive agriculture. Farmers should, proposed Clements, work with rather than against the land, adopting those practices which most closely resembled the natural succession and its tried and tested adaptation to the prevailing conditions. Clements's call for more intelligent and sensitive land use and the notion of the natural climax as an 'ideal state' against which man-modified habitats might be compared was, albeit implictly, a moral position.

Tansley found this intrusion of ethics into ecological debate highly objectionable. Modern man, he argued, was an integral part of the landscape and there was no difference at all between a natural climax and an artificial or 'anthropogenic' one. Indeed there could be a proliferation of different climaxes side by side, all of which were, from a moral standpoint, equally acceptable. Tansley argued that 'we cannot confine ourselves to the so-called natural entities and ignore the processes and expression of vegetation now so abundantly provided us by the activities of man', continuing:

> ... it is obvious that modern civilised man upsets the "natural" ecosystems or "biotic communities" on a very large scale... Regarded as an exceptionally powerful biotic factor which increasingly upsets the equilibrium of pre-existing ecosystems and eventually destroys

them, at the same time forming new ones of very different nature, human activity finds its proper place in ecology.

Tansley's views were therefore entirely in line with those of Oliver. Ecology's task was to assist man in the efficient exploitation of natural resources. 'We cannot arrest the progressive adaptation of the country to human needs, nor should we try to do so if we could', he wrote, arguing that ecology was 'an essential part of the scientific foundation of forestry and the management of grasslands'. It therefore represented 'the solution to many of the great economic problems which face the modern world'. From this perspective ecology was little more than a division of economics, a provider of scientific advice to the business of forestry and agriculture.

This thinking was very much in tune with the 'progressive' movement in America. Here, the 'scientific conservation' or 'wise use' philosophy which came to prominence under Theodore Roosevelt sought to place natural resources under a strict managerial regime for the greater economic good of the nation. In this context the notion of a Clementsian 'yardstick' against which man's actions could be unfavourably measured was not only scientifically flawed. It represented a threat to the very legitimacy of the human assault on nature.

Tansley's criticisms of Clements, and later of his South African colleague John Phillips, were freely aired and took on the form of a highly public row, the consequences of which were to echo around Anglo-American ecological debate for years. These divergent views were perhaps inevitable, however. Clements could hardly ignore the ploughing up of America's pristine native grassland which was going on right outside his door or the subsequent devastating consequences of the 'Dust Bowl'. Tansley, by contrast, lived in a country where any approximation of a natural climax condition lay buried deep in the past. Most of Britain's landscape was the product of long human presence and manipulation, the result of which was a subtle and complex natural and human landscape which was, at least until the agricultural revolution which followed the Second War, still regarded by most as both aesthetically pleasing and biologically diverse. The nation's most valued plants and animals had arisen, argued Tansley, not through natural succession but through man's prevention of the process.

The clash between Tansley and Clements was far from a new schism, however. Clements was no environmentalist but he nevertheless found himself with at least one foot in a deep-rooted and radically different intellectual tradition, one which rejected science's more hard-edged, utilitarian tendencies in favour of a more subjective, respectful and morally-inclined view of nature. Though it had identifiable roots in Britain, this was to become a predominantly American vision.

Gilbert White's The *Natural History of Selborne* presents a pastoral, arcadian picture of rural England. Here we see a holistic, inclusive vision of the natural world in which man is but a humble part. White's work represents perhaps the first, halting articulation of an ecological viewpoint but it also represents the beginnings of a discernably 'biocentric' approach and a whole new tradition of environmental thinking.

Such notions were most fully explored in the New World in the writings of the naturalist-philosopher Henry David Thoreau. Around his home in Concord, Massachusetts, he noted, like White, a myriad of natural interdependencies: 'In Nature nothing is wasted. Every decayed leaf and twig and fibre is only the better fitted to serve in some other department'. He recognised the Grey Squirrel for 'the great service it performs, in the economy of the universe'. But Thoreau was most concerned with man's place in nature. In his 1851 essay *Walking* he argues that we must also 'regard man as an inhabitant, or a part and parcel of nature'. He calls for an acceptance of nature's lessons and a more sensitive accommodation to its rhythms. 'Would it not be well', he argues, 'to consult with Nature in the outset for she is the most extensive and experienced planter of us all'.

For Oliver and Tansley such ideas would have been interesting history at best but in the 1930s, at the height of Tansley's disagreements with Clements, a new incarnation of these old ideas began to emerge. This time, however, it came not from a country parson or a misanthropic outsider but from an insider, a respected member of the scientific establishment. His name was Aldo Leopold.

For much of his early career with the American Forest Service Leopold was a strong advocate, like Oliver and Tansley, of the 'scientific management' of nature. Ecology, he argued, was 'the outstanding discovery of the twentieth century'. In time, however, he was to turn against 'economic conservation' and its premise that the natural world existed purely to serve economic ends. Scarred by his experience of the ecological consequences of 'game management' in America's Southwest, he began to articulate an alternative ecology, a rival vision of what this new science might represent.

In 1935 he moved to a shack in the 'sand counties' of Wisconsin. Here his ideas began to develop further and in 1949, a year after his death, came the posthumous publication of *A Sand County Almanac*, his defining collection of essays. His call in this work for a 'land ethic' was an explicit argument for a new relationship with the natural world:

> When we see land as a community to which we belong, we may begin to use it with love and respect... That land is a community is a basic concept of ecology, but that land is to be loved and respected is an extension of ethics.

Recognising the ethical connections and obligations which are already implicit in our social and economic affairs, Leopold suggests that 'the land ethic simply enlarges the boundaries of the community to include soils, waters, plants and animals, or collectively: the land'. In a clear echo of Clements, Leopold regarded wild land as a means of measuring the damage done to the wider environment. Wild places, he argues 'reveal what the land was, what it is, and what it ought to be'.

Here was a new biocentric philosophy, a coherent countervision to the hard rationality of the ecological establishment on both sides of the Atlantic and a new more humble and ethical direction for ecology. Leopold's environmental ethic was an intellectual milestone, arguably one of the most important ideas of the twentieth century, but, although it was revolutionary in its thinking, *A Sand County Almanac* exerted little immediate influence over the development of this new science, either in America or in Europe. Although ecology had a new prophet, few were listening.

The route which ecology was to take in the post-war world remained instead firmly in the mould set by Tansley in Britain and by his 'progressive' contemporaries in America. Though a biocentric, arcadian version of ecology has been embraced by the amateur naturalist and has become the central organising idea for the modern conservation movement, Tansley's version has been most influential. The so-called 'new ecology' has extended its remit beyond plants and animals to include the planet's other components, its soils, its rocks and its gases, its basic 'ingredients'. Today ecology has become closely allied not just to economics but to physics, its language one of 'living capital', 'energy flows' and 'productivity'. It has become ever more preoccupied with measurement, an essentially mathematical enterprise but one still based on the old ethos, the unchallenged premise that nature needs to be managed. This is nature removed from the ethical realm altogether, envisioned as little more than a factory, ordered by flowchart and overseen by men in white coats.

It is now over a century since Oliver, Tansley and Clements walked together on Blakeney Point. Since then the Point has continued to change, its ecological successions proceeding unchecked, an endless process of trial and error, colonisation and extinction, advance and retreat. The vegetation has continued to shift, adapting to the ridge's movement and to the forces of accretion and erosion. Some plant species have disappeared, whilst new colonists have arrived, borne here by wind or sea or brought by birds.

These successions and 'disruptions' at Blakeney Point are of course (with the exception of Oliver's introductions) entirely natural. They stand in stark contrast to the changes now wrought across the wider countryside. The 1947 Agriculture Act saw the beginning of modern farming and a lasting impact on Britain's countryside. The effect of mechanisation, crop monocultures, pesticides, autumn sowing and the loss of hedgerows and field margins has been catastrophic. Informed by ecology's new insights, post-war industrial agriculture has transformed Britain's rural landscape and decimated its native flora and fauna. Today it is difficult to support Tansley's proposition that ecology is morally ambivalent, that all change is morally neutral. Some changes, most would now agree, are worse than others.

Despite Tansley's rejection of the idea, Blakeney Point acts as a ready 'yardstick', a reminder of what a naturally-functioning ecosystem looks like. It continues to provide a textbook case study in vegetational succession and ecological change but it also invites us to reflect on this still young science, on who controls its definition and direction and on what ends it should serve. Above all, it asks us how we see nature, how we value it and what our place in the natural order should be.

4

NATURE IN TRUST

It is generally agreed that unspoiled sea coast is a particularly precious possession.

Arthur Tansley

The notion of the 'nature reserve' was slow to take hold in Britain. The protection of green space for recreation and the preservation of historic sites and buildings dominated early thinking. Perhaps surprisingly, therefore, Blakeney Point was to become one of Britain's earliest reserves and the first to be on the coast. This came about largely through the action of the Point's ecologists who sought to protect this place not because of its appeal as landscape or its wildlife importance but because of its potential as a scientific laboratory. Such ideas went on to dominate national thinking, the 'Blakeney Point ecologists' occupying key positions of influence in framing the ideas behind the planning of Britain's post-war network of statutory scientific reserves.

Plate 7. The Laboratory and the Plantation (*Andy Stoddart*)

Plate 8. Arthur Tansley

2012 saw the centenary of the National Trust's acquisition of Blakeney Point and a series of associated celebrations to mark the event. Blakeney Point is, however, no ordinary nature reserve. Almost none have a longer history and none are today so decorated with conservation designations. The Point is, or falls within, a National Nature Reserve, a Natural Area, a Site of Special Scientific Interest, a Special Area of Conservation, a Special Protection Area, a Biosphere reserve, a Ramsar site, an Area of Outstanding Natural Beauty and a Heritage Coast.

So familiar have some of these terms become that we can be forgiven for thinking that we have always had nature reserves. Today the notion of a special site protected for its wildlife importance seems entirely uncontroversial. From today's perspective it seems that we have always thought about wild places this way and that the acquisition of Blakeney Point as a nature reserve was simply part of an enlightened drive to preserve the best of our natural heritage. We might even allow ourselves a little self-congratulation on our collective vision and foresight as a nation. But such satisfaction would be premature. Behind the celebration of our progress in protecting wild nature lies another much more complicated history. The nature reserve, it turns out, is not such an old idea at all. Nor is the concept and purpose of the nature reserve even universally understood.

To earlier generations, the idea that agriculture and settlement were things to be resisted would have been extraordinary. What better measure was there of man's civilisation than the clearance of the forests, the cultivation of the land and the building of towns and villages? Agriculture was the definition of civilisation, the very process which turned nature into culture. Man's unquestioned duty was to tame and subdue the earth, to cut down the wildwood, plough the grasslands and drain the marshes. Kings might set aside forests and deer parks as their own private hunting reserves but to do so for any other purpose, so that non-game birds and mammals could be protected, would have been an absurd idea.

Eventually, the Industrial Revolution heralded a rapid growth of towns and cities and ever greater landscape transformation. Despite these wholesale changes to the landscape, however, little threat to the natural fabric was perceived. The earliest priority of nature conservation in Britain was the protection not of habitats but of species, almost invariably birds.

This latter aim would, thought most, be best achieved through legislation. The notion of a nature reserve, an area set aside for the protection of all its flora and fauna, hardly registered, even in the thoughts of the most ardent protectionists. Reserves, it was widely agreed, would be too expensive to acquire and maintain and, once established, would only attract the attention of those they were intended to hold at bay. Legislation and a change in attitudes would be enough. Nature could then be left to look after itself.

These ideas were in sharp contrast to those being played out in America. Here voices were raised to protect at least some of the new continent's natural riches before they were destroyed by the plough and the axe. As early as 1841 the artist George Catlin had called for the creation of 'a magnificent park' to protect the Plains grasslands and their native culture. In mid-century Henry David Thoreau had famously argued that 'in wildness is the preservation of the world'. By the 1870s the exploration of the West had opened the nation's eyes to the scenic wonders of the Rockies and, stirred by the monumental Romantic paintings of Thomas Moran and the impassioned wilderness advocacy of John Muir, Yellowstone became America's first National Park in 1872.

There were, however, no equivalent voices here in England. Here there was no perceived threat to the wilderness. Indeed there was little true wilderness left to protect. The legacy of England's long history of human occupation was a landscape which had always accommodated itself to man's presence. England's countryside was an artificial landscape but one which, through traditional land use practices, had preserved a relatively rich and diverse wildlife. The notion of a nature reserve, a land set aside specifically for wildlife, therefore carried little logic. In England, therefore, the first calls for the preservation of land came not from artists or naturalist-philosophers but from an entirely different direction.

By the nineteenth century England had become a fully industrialised nation. Naturally, the rich maintained their country estates but most people now lived in towns and cities. Here they experienced not just a physical distancing from nature but also a spiritual estrangement, and pressure soon grew for access to green space for public recreation. This led to the establishment in 1865 of a Commons Preservation Society and the battle was quickly waged to protect sites such as Hampstead Heath and Epping Forest for all to enjoy.

The key figures in this movement were the solicitor and civil servant Robert Hunter and the social reform campaigner Octavia Hill. Hunter was quick to see the need to create a statutory body to acquire and hold land for public use and as early as 1865 it was agreed to call such a body the 'National Trust'. Only modest progress towards this goal was made, however, until in 1885 their paths crossed those of Canon Hardwicke Rawnsley, the countryside campaigner and celebrated defender of the Lake District. Finally, on 12th January 1895, the 'National Trust for Places of Historic Interest or Natural Beauty' was registered, founded to act as custodian of property given to the nation. The 1907 National Trust Act which formally recognised its statutory role also contained an important clause allowing the Trust to declare its property inalienable, unable to be sold, mortgaged or given away. The Trust's objects, as enshrined in the Act, were:

> ... to promote the permanent preservation, for the benefit of the Nation, of lands and tenements (including buildings) of beauty or historic interest; and as regards land, to preserve (so far as practicable) their natural aspect, features, and animal and plant life.

These words are revealing. They represent a clear shift away from an explicit focus on access to green spaces as public amenity and towards a new emphasis on historic sites, particularly historic buildings. In the references to 'beauty' and 'animal and plant life' lies a recognition of other values and ambitions too but the precise order of priorities amongst these objectives is unclear. Although by 1910 the Trust owned around a dozen properties of natural history importance, nature conservation was not the main focus of its work and its objectives provided no charter for the creation of nature reserves as we might understand them today.

The nation's first recognisable nature reserve had been created in 1813 by the famously eccentric naturalist and South American explorer Charles Waterton. In between his expeditions he erected an eight-foot-high wall around his estate at Walton Hall, near Wakefield, and banned hunting within its perimeter. He declared that his estate was now a nature reserve, put up nestboxes and ordered his gamekeeper to desist from shooting predators.

This was, by the standards of the time, a somewhat eccentric thing to do and Waterton's actions were regarded with widespread incredulity and incomprehension. However, as the century progressed, a tiny handful of individuals and groups began to act on behalf of other sites. Perhaps the most notable event was the purchase of Norfolk's Breydon Water in 1888 by the Breydon Society.

By the turn of the century, however, a new voice was calling not just for an isolated reserve here or there but for a whole network of reserves right across the country. A prominent banker and entomologist, Nathaniel Charles Rothschild articulated a whole new vision of nature conservation, arguing for the protection not just of individual species but also of their habitats. Rothschild was clear: legislation and education would not, in themselves, preserve Britain's wildlife. It was also necessary to buy land.

However, although encouraged by the work of the National Trust, Rothschild was frustrated with the reactive nature of its acquisitions. With no plan to secure the best sites, the Trust merely acquired whatever came its way and was not actively involved in seeking protection for the most important and vulnerable areas. As a result, Rothschild and three colleagues formed the Society for the Promotion of Nature Reserves in 1912, partly to obtain the support of wealthy and influential individuals of the time. Naturally, Rothschild's personal wealth and wider connections placed him in an ideal position to undertake this role but he often put up the money himself, purchasing both Wicken Fen in Cambridgeshire and Woodwalton Fen in Huntingdonshire.

But there was also another motivation behind the formation of the SPNR. This was to put pressure on the National Trust. Its aim was not to own land itself but to identify and survey those sites most in need of protection, to raise funds for their acquisition and then to hand them over to the Trust for ongoing management.

There was, perhaps inevitably, a tension between the National Trust and the SPNR. This had already come to a head when Rothschild had tried to hand over Woodwalton Fen but it had been refused due to its high management costs and on the grounds that it was 'only of interest to the naturalist'. Instead Woodwalton Fen was given to the SPNR, although Rothschild also had to provide the means to pay for its ongoing management. Despite Rothschild's view of its strategic deficiencies, however, the Trust was still regarded as the best body to act as recipient of land. It had special privileges granted by Parliament, greater resources and growing experience of land management.

Rothschild was also very careful to forge links with the leading scientific figures of the day, and the inclusion on the SPNR Council of Arthur Tansley, Edward Salisbury and, as the representative of the National Trust, Francis Oliver, goes a long way towards explaining the first significant acquisition facilitated by Rothschild's new organisation.

With the death of the sixth Lord Calthorpe in 1911, his entire estate on the north Norfolk coast, including Blakeney Point, came onto the market. Agreement had already been reached with Oliver for the Point to be used for 'marine horticulture' (the study of botany) and further agreement was now reached for it to be sold as a separate lot. With the finances provided by an anonymous benefactor (Rothschild of course) and a smaller contribution from the Fishmongers' Company, the Point was sold to Alexander Crundall of Surbiton, Surrey, then transferred to the National Trust in August 1912 to become its forty-ninth acquisition and its first coastal property. Indeed Blakeney Point was the first coastal nature reserve in the country.

Oliver's role was key. He led a public appeal for funds and his position on both the Executive Committee of the National Trust and the Council of the SPNR ensured that the Trust accepted his recommendation to acquire Blakeney Point. Until this point the Trust's focus had been on buildings, ancient monuments and sites with high historical or cultural importance and, given the Point's obvious deficiencies in these areas, it should clearly have been turned down. Furthermore, the Trust, and indeed the wider public, showed little enthusiasm at the time for coastal landscapes. However, Oliver's emphasis of the Point's value as a scientific laboratory carried the day. The Trust's Provisional Council clearly took the point, noting that:

> To the ornithologist, the botanist and physiographist, Blakeney is a veritable treasure; it is a resting-place for summer migrants and hundreds of birds may be seen here, the plant-life is of peculiar interest, while the formation of the shingle beaches and dunes with the curious 'hooks' afford an admirable illustration of the action of wind and waves.

Following its acquisition, the Executive Committee of the Trust agreed to allow Oliver and UCL to continue with their work and to build a laboratory there in 1913. The Trust also agreed to take on responsibility for the Watcher, Bob Pinchen.

In acquiring Blakeney Point, the National Trust had broken the mould. It had agreed to take over and manage a property not to protect a historic site or building nor for any clearly stated desire to protect public amenity or natural beauty but for a much more utilitarian reason: to protect its value to the scientific community as an outdoor laboratory and research facility. This was a wholly new direction for the Trust, its 1912 Report noting that 'the Council... feels that this may be the beginning of what may eventually prove to be an important development of the work of the Trust and may enable it to enlist the sympathies of naturalists and scientists'.

In its 1913 Report, however, the Trust's Council appears to shift its ground again, this time towards a more overtly environmental philosophy:

> It is hoped that the acquisition of this property (Blakeney Point) by the National Trust may be the beginning of a larger movement in the direction of preserving areas through the country, which may be regarded as reserves for wild nature.

This idea of what a nature reserve could be was picked up in a contemporary article on the purchase published in *The Times*:

> It is hoped that with Blakeney Point a satisfactory beginning of the establishment of natural reserves may be made in England, and it is appropriate that the body which has been selected to hold the property should be the National Trust for Places of Historic Interest or Natural Beauty, for, quite apart from its appeal to the scientist and naturalist, Blakeney Point is a beautiful open space with its long stretches of yellow sand and windswept dunes.

Although such aesthetic sentiments went well beyond those articulated by the Trust at the time, it was clear that the acquisition of Blakeney Point had sown the seeds for a whole new direction for nature conservation in England. These seeds, however, would take a long time to germinate. Only in 1938, with the creation of a Coastal Preservation Committee, did the protection of the coast become a central mission of the Trust.

Following the purchase of Blakeney Point, the SPNR continued to compile its 'shopping list' of sites for potential nature reserves. This was completed in 1915 and listed over 250 sites in three categories. 'Category A' sites were generally large and typical representatives of their ecological type, sites in 'Category B' were generally smaller, the home of unique or local species, whilst those in 'Catgeory C' were other sites deemed not to be in immediate danger. Rothschild was the first to draw up such a list and to attempt to distinguish between various categories of importance. He also gave careful attention to the international context, emphasising those habitat types which were particularly well represented in Britain, such as sand dunes, shingle beaches and saltmarshes.

Rothschild's list was duly sent to the Board of Agriculture but little happened as a result. Not even the National Trust used the list as the basis of its acquisitions and indeed continued to refuse ownership of some reserves, arguing still that some were of interest only to naturalists. Moreover, the First War had shifted the national attention away from any embryonic interest in nature conservation. It had also prematurely curtailed the operation of the SPNR. Rothschild himself fell ill in 1918 and died in 1923. With its founder dead, the SPNR's vision and drive largely disappeared. Relying on its contacts with the wealthy, the Society had no mass membership on which to draw for political or financial support and, inevitably, it struggled for influence. Although it limped on as an organisation, its subsequent achievements were modest.

In this context, the acquisition of Blakeney Point stands out, not as the dawning of a bright new age for nature conservation but as a happy accident, a fortuitous conjunction of people and events. The majority opinion still opposed the acquisition of reserves. The RSPB, for example, rejected a public appeal for funds to acquire land at Dungeness in Kent because 'its birds and desolation would not appeal to the British public in the least, but only to a limited number of people who care about fauna and wild places'.

The idea of the nature reserve was not completely abandoned, however, and a few far-sighted individuals and voluntary groups continued to press for their creation. In Northumberland, the Farne Islands Association raised funds in 1923 to purchase the islands and their important colonies of terns and seals and hand them over to the National Trust. In the same year another key acquisition was made in north Norfolk.

Only ten or so miles to the west of Blakeney Point lies Scolt Head Island. A long, mobile shingle ridge crowned with dunes, it shares remarkable similarities with the Point and was quickly recognised as an equally important site for scientific study. Key to the acquisition of Scolt Head and its subsequent handover to the National Trust was Dr. Sydney Long, a Norwich Doctor (though born in Wells) and Honorary Secretary of the Norfolk and Norwich Naturalists' Society. Long and Oliver worked together to arrange the island's purchase by public subscription on behalf of the NNNS and the island (bar a small section at its eastern end) was then handed over to the Trust.

The example set by the purchase of Blakeney Point and now Scolt Head inspired further developments in north Norfolk. Shortly afterwards, the death of A.W. Cozens-Hardy of Cley Hall precipitated the sale of 407 acres of Cley grazing marshes. Lying immediately to the east of Blakeney Point, their potential value in protecting an even greater and more diverse area was obvious. In a speech in Cley's George Hotel (once the favoured haunt of the gentlemen gunners) Long noted that:

> When one considers the changes in the face of the country that are being made or contemplated by Forestry Commission, Drainage Boards, speculative builders and the like, one is anxious to preserve for future generations areas of marsh, heath, woods and undrained fenland... with their natural wealth of flora and fauna.

Long was successful in raising the £5,160 necessary to secure the purchase but recognised the need for a trust to be established to own and manage the land. He therefore established the Norfolk Naturalists' Trust in 1926, the first of its kind in the country. Amongst its founding objectives were 'to protect areas of natural beauty or scientific interest' and 'to establish and maintain reserves' and this new organisation went on to acquire a further seven sites by the 1940s. Oliver was enthusiastic about these develoments. He saw that here 'we have the germ which may lead to far-reaching results', noting that 'if the enterprise succeeded one would look forward to the time when every county would have its County trust which would hold and administer the areas it acquired'.

Perhaps surprisingly, E.C. Arnold was also a strong advocate of nature reserves, purchasing a disused brickpit, a wood and some marshland near his home in Sussex and, at Salthouse, a section of marsh immediately to the east of Cley. On his death, this area was handed over to the National Trust and remains known to this day as 'Arnold's Marsh'. In his 1940 book *Bird Reserves* he sets out his own ideas on conservation:

> To my mind bird protection nowadays is far more a matter of preserving bird haunts than of making laws to protect birds, which may easily, like the Kentish plover, be exterminated by progress... the only wild land ultimately saved will be that which we have saved ourselves.

Arnold was right. Nature reserves were only being created by the action of enlightened individuals and groups. There was no national drive for their creation or consensus over what they should be for and, although events in north Norfolk had demonstrated what could be achieved, the idea of the nature reserve made little progress elsewhere.

In the inter-war years most continued to see conservation not as a means of safeguarding nature but as a matter of preserving land for public access. The countryside's greatest value, argued most, lay in its role as amenity, providing relaxation, recreation and a pleasant green space for the town-dweller. Increasing leisure time fuelled a renewed demand for access to the countryside, reflected in the founding of the Youth Hostels Association in 1930 and the Ramblers' Association in 1935 and also in the famous Kinder Scout trespass of 1932.

The 'big idea' to address this need was a network of 'National Parks'. These could not just be imitations of those in America, however. Here there were no untouched natural wildernesses which could be owned outright by Government. National Parks in Britain would have to accommodate themselves to a landscape which was only semi-natural and which was already occupied and worked. Eventually, after the Second War, an initial network of ten National Parks was created, all in the open upland areas of the north and west.

Naturalists and those concerned with conserving nature were not, however, generally part of such discussions. The notions of nature as public amenity and nature as something to be protected remained entirely separate and, at least during the 1930s, the amenity lobby had both the loudest voice and the ear of the politicians. The inter-war years were all about access to the countryside, not about nature conservation.

Only in the 1940s did the country catch up with Rothschild and his ideas. In preparing strategies for post-war reconstruction, the Government finally recognised that it had a role in the planning of future land use. At first the threat to the countryside was perceived by most to come from industrialisation and the spread of the cities and their suburbs. Indeed it was often expressed in terms of a threat to farmland. Even in 1945 Tansley still considered that 'the great extension of agriculture during the war has not on the whole diminished the beauty of the countryside: rather the contrary is true'. 'It is scarcely probable', he wrote, 'that the extension of agriculture will go much further, for the limits of agricultural land must have been reached in most places'. For a while the National Trust also rejected any notion of a conflict between conservation and progressive agriculture. A tidy, prosperous landscape was, it argued, more pleasing on the eye and a better public amenity. Eventually, however, most came to accept that changes in land use and management could also be major threats to wildlife.

Forestry had already begun to transform the nation's landscape. Woodland had previously been managed through traditional, 'low intensity' practices such as coppicing but after the First War forestry had become a business charged with national timber production targets. The Forestry Commission was set up 1919 and by 1939 nearly half a million acres were afforested. Rows of introduced exotic conifers now marched across the landscape, planted as a cash crop with little thought to their impact on wildlife or the countryside.

By contrast, farmers had always been regarded as custodians of the natural landscape but the war-time pressure on food supply had led to unprecedented landscape change. Across the country grassland and heathland had been ploughed and wetlands drained and in the dash for ever greater efficiency traditional countryside features such as natural flood meadows had almost disappeared. Although less visually intrusive than urbanisation and afforestation, new agricultural practices presented, in reality, an even greater threat to wildlife.

Nature reserves had once been regarded as special places for the protection of rare species but now, in this new context, at least some realised that the 'common' species could not be relied upon to survive in an increasingly artificial and intensively managed countryside. Conserving nature was no longer a matter of protecting a few sites for the rarest species but of protecting as many sites as possible.

To make sense of this new context the SPNR convened a conference in 1941 under the banner 'Nature Preservation in Post-War Reconstruction'. It led to the setting up by Government in 1942 of a Nature Reserves Investigation Committee 'to report on the types and approximate areas of reserves and sanctuaries which should be provided and the localities where they should be situated'. Finally Government had realised that it had a role in the protection of land and habitats as well as in the passing of legislation to protect species. The establishment of nature reserves would now receive the attention previously devoted to the creation of National Parks.

By far the loudest voices in this process were those of the ecologists. They had already been instrumental in the acquisition of Blakeney Point. Now, in the new national appetite for nature reserves, they sensed a further opportunity. However, as with Blakeney Point, their interest in establishing reserves was not for reasons of landscape quality or wildlife value. Their priority was to acquire those locations best suited to scientific research. Of course, by 'research' they meant the study of nature in pursuit of economic objectives. Indeed Oliver had previously argued that the land area devoted to nature reserves should be small so as to maximise production on as much of the nation's 'waste land' as possible. Whilst the protection of species was being driven by the warmth of public sentiment, therefore, that of habitats was being steered by the much colder vision of a scientific elite.

Oliver was by now in Egypt but Tansley and Salisbury held significant positions of influence, notably on the SPNR Council and the National Trust Executive Committee. While serving on the latter, Tansley had argued strongly for 'scientific interest' to be added to the Trust's objects. The British Ecological Society was also anxious to ensure that, in selecting any reserves, the scientific viewpoint would prevail and, to this end, Salisbury was put forward as a member of the NRIC. In 1943 the BES also set up its own committee, with Tansley as its Chairman and Salisbury as a member, and in the same year published *Nature Conservation in Britain*, a prospectus for the role of ecology in the selection of nature reserves.

Tansley became the most enthusiastic publicist for the nature reserve idea, publishing in 1945 his own book *Our Heritage of Wild Nature: A Plea for Organized Nature Conservation.* Here, in what amounts to a personal manifesto, the ideas which were most influential in proposing the nation's first nature reserves are clearly set out.

Tansley is clear first of all that this is a job for Government, noting in his first chapter that 'some kind of public action will... be the only means by which rural beauty can be preserved' and that 'decisions will have to be made by a public authority'. Tansley had little faith in voluntary organisations such as the National Trust to act in a sufficiently strategic and scientifically-informed manner and he looked to Government for leadership.

Initially he couches his thesis in aesthetic terms, arguing that if industrialisation and suburban spread continue unchecked 'without regard to the preservation of the beauty and character of our landscapes, the result must be a land that will have lost the greater part of its rural charm'. Further arguments are mounted in respect of the amenity and educational value of the countryside but Tansley's thesis quickly centres on its value as a place for scientific research:

> It is essential to the work of ecologists that large samples of the natural and semi-natural vegetation of the country should be maintained in order that they may study what nature does under given conditions of climate and soil and the influence of man.

Blakeney Point features prominently in this publication for it combines in one site three of the habitat types - sand dune, shingle and saltmarsh - regarded by Tansley as most worthy of protection. The Point is cited as a prime example of how amenity, educational and scientific interests can be compatible. It is, he notes, an 'almost ideal example of public enjoyment with facilities for scientific and educational work'.

Eventually the BES committee merged with the NRIC and in 1945 a list of forty-seven 'National Nature Reserves' was proposed together with twenty-five 'conservation areas'. The work of the NRIC was then taken forward by a new Wild Life Conservation Special Committee, chaired initially by Julian Huxley and subsequently by Tansley.

The new committee published its report, entitled *Conservation of Nature in England and Wales*, in 1947, adopting most of the recommendations of the NRIC and expanding the list of proposed reserves to seventy-three. The report also proposed the creation of thirty-five 'scientific areas' as well as the establishment of local education reserves by local authorities and the protection of geological monuments.

Here was a clear prospectus for the future. Whilst the National Parks would focus on access and amenity, the new National Nature Reserves would be for the study and protection of habitats and species. Most of the committee's recommendations were taken forward in the 1949 National Parks and Access to the Countryside Act but the concept of 'scientific areas' was replaced by that of the 'Site of Special Scientific Interest' to provide some protection for sites outside the statutory reserves. In the words of the Act, the National Nature Reserves would provide:

> ... under suitable conditions and control, special opportunities for the study of, and research into, matters relating to the fauna and flora of Great Britain and the physical conditions in which they live, and for the study of geographical and physiographical features of special interest in the area, or preserving flora, fauna or geographical or physiographical features of special interest in the area.

Despite nods in the direction of species and habitat protection, the overriding rationale for these developments was scientific. Both the NRIC and the Huxley Committee were clear that reserves should be set up mainly for their scientific value, and this emphasis was duly enshrined in the Act. Nature conservation was now firmly in the hands of the ecologists, its declared purpose the preservation of habitats and wildlife for their scientific value and to protect field evidence for ecological research. The new reserves were no mere refuge for wildlife, they were an outdoor workshop for the ecologist.

A further important recommendation was the establishment of a 'biological service' as a Government body to select and acquire reserves, carry out surveys and research, manage the nominated sites and advise local and national Government on conservation issues. As a result, the 1949 Act created the Nature Conservancy, an ecological research body to oversee and support the establishment of the new network of reserves. Tansley was appointed as its first Chairman. The objectives of the new body were:

> ... to provide scientific advice on the conservation and control of the natural flora and fauna of Great Britain; to establish, maintain and manage nature reserves in Great Britain, including the maintenance of physical features of scientific interest; and to organise and develop the research and scientific services related thereto.

The ecologists were therefore clear that their job didn't stop with the designation or acquisition of reserves. Conservation meant not a 'hands off' relationship with nature but an active process of regulation and control. Tansley's prime focus is, of course, on plants but In *Our Heritage of Wild Nature* he also writes of animals, arguing that 'we need thorough knowledge of their habits, their special modes of life and their fluctuating numbers, if we are to devise the right methods of regulation'. He continues:

> Man has long ago upset the *natural* balance, and he has to establish a new one which is consonant with his own interests. To do this he must *regulate* the populations of the different animals, exterminating some and conserving others, reducing populations here, encouraging them there.

'Regulation and control are essential', Tansley proposes, 'because some of the animals, under existing conditions, are harmful to human interests'. Reserve acquisition was to be just the prelude to an ongoing, scientifically controlled programme of habitat manipulation to ensure the protection of the most prized plant and animal communities and the elimination of those deemed harmful. The former had arisen, argued Tansley, because of traditional land use practices which had stopped natural succession from taking place and so created a wide variety of niches for a greater variety of species. On the new reserves nature couldn't be left to run riot. It needed the attention of trained scientists.

This stance had enormous implications, not just in terms of the choices to be made in this ecological manipulation, over which species to favour at the expense of others, but also in terms of the management and financial resources necessary to continue this task. The nature reserve warden, it seemed, would become not a guardian of pristine wilderness but a reinvented gamekeeper.

Tansley died in 1955, by which time his vision was largely in place: a system of National Nature Reserves identified and actively managed according to strict ecological criteria. Since the Tansley era the development of nature reserves has continued at least partly in this mould. The number of National Nature Reserves has continued to grow, some purchased or acquired on long-term lease, others subject to shorter-term management agreements with landowners, and over three thousand SSSIs have now been designated.

But the idea of the nature reserve has also developed in new directions. The science-led and Government-backed approach to conservation created an entirely new context for the voluntary bodies and they were quick to spot new opportunities to supplement and complement the statutory reserve network. Furthermore, with changing aesthetic tastes and an increasing public appreciation of wild landscapes (including coastlines), it soon became possible to protect land not just because it was scientifically interesting or economically useful but because it had scenic quality or wildlife value.

After its reluctant start, the RSPB has become a significant landowner. Only ten reserves were in place by 1960 but the pace of acquisitions increased significantly in the 1970s and it now manages a portfolio of around 150 properties.

In 1965, over fifty years after its acquisition of Blakeney Point for scientific reasons, the National Trust launched its Enterprise Neptune programme, aimed at protecting Britain's remaining stretches of undeveloped and unspoiled coast. By the end of the 1980s it had purchased or acquired an additional five hundred miles, including, in 1973, the saltmarshes at Morston and, in 1976, those at Stiffkey.

Perhaps the most dramatic development, however, has been the growth of the local Wildlife Trusts movement. Today, a network of forty-seven Trusts covers the entire country, owns and manages hundreds of nature reserves and has an increasingly powerful voice through the Wildlife Trusts coordinating body, the inheritor of Rothschild's SPNR.

The centenary of Blakeney Point's ground-breaking acquisition therefore provides an opportunity to reflect on what has been achieved. There is of course much to celebrate: a clear Government commitment to nature reserves and a thriving network of voluntary organisations with ever-greater land holdings. The idea of the nature reserve now has universal support and nature tourism, often built around reserves, is increasingly valuable to local economies. On these measures, Britain is the envy of the world.

However, although the number of reserves continues to grow, the network of SSSIs has been extensively damaged and the impact on the wider countryside has been severe. There is an increasing gulf between the ecological value of reserves and that of the wider countryside.

Many old questions therefore remain. What are today's nature reserves for? Should they be a last retreat for rare species or should we be more concerned about the wider countryside where most of our 'common' species reside? Can any reserves be left untouched or should there always be active intervention on behalf of certain species? If the latter, which are the priorities and which are expendable? What roles do scientific research, education and recreation have?

And there are new questions too. Can reserves be 'bridgeheads' from which rare species might re-enter the wider environment? Can reserves be enlarged and connected to form 'corridors' or more extensive 'living landscapes'? Should the focus be on restoring and recreating vanished habitats?

A hundred years ago Blakeney Point led the way in developing one idea of what the nature reserve might be. In the post-war era, its ecologists went on to frame the ideas behind a statutory network of scientific reserves. Today, in a new context, Blakeney Point continues to pose questions about what reserves should be, who they might be for and how they might best be managed.

5

SHIFTING GROUND

It is not down in any map; true places never are.

Herman Melville

Blakeney Point was, however, not just an outdoor laboratory for ecologists. It was also discovered by coastal geographers who quickly recognised that it provided a classic case study in the development of shingle spits, dunes and saltmarshes. This work nurtured the wholly new science of coastal geomorphology and added greatly to our knowledge of mobile, shifting coastlines but it also played into much older ideas, challenging our traditional notions of landscape permanence. These ideas came to a head in the infamous 'storm surge' of 31st January 1953. The interplay of land and sea was now no longer only of interest to academics. For all who live by the sea it had a new significance, one with even greater resonance today.

Plate 9. Aerial view of Blakeney Point (*Mike Page*)

Plate 10. Young dunes on the outer beach (*Andy Stoddart*)

The main shingle ridge of Blakeney Point is made up of billions of pieces of flint. Their smoothly-rounded shapes fit perfectly in the hand and they have a pleasing heaviness and coolness against the palm. They are objects of beauty too, their soft matt exteriors glowing with the soft reflected light of a Vermeer. Cool dove-greys, chalky whites and deep ink-blues dominate but there is a myriad of other hues too: lavender, tan, ruby, ochre, peat, ivory and rust.

This vast accumulation of shingle begins at Weybourne Hope, where a steeply-shelving beach and deep water have long offered a tempting prospect to smugglers and would-be invaders. However, this point on the coast also marks a significant transition in the landscape. Here the nature of the shoreline changes dramatically. To the east lie two-tone cliffs of yellowish-white chalk and mud-coloured sand, gravel and clay, whose eroding ramparts slowly but steadily reclaim the fields behind. West from here, however, the chalk dips below the surface, the horizon flattens and the shore is marked only by a long strip of shingle.

Though the orientation of the Norfolk coast now runs due west from here all the way to the Wash, this shingle ridge turns outward at a slight angle. For its first four miles it runs straight and narrow, separating the sea from what was once an estuary but now takes the form of reclaimed marshes threaded with reed-fringed dykes, patrolled by stiff-winged Marsh Harriers and grazed by cattle. Then, opposite the village of Cley, the ridge leaves the reclaimed land behind and for another four miles it becomes an isolated shingle spit, enclosing on its inland flank the villages of Blakeney and Morston, a great expanse of glistening intertidal mud and the eastern end of England's greatest saltmarsh.

From the end of the Cley beach road, the shingle is steep on its seaward face but more gently sloping on its inland side. After almost a mile the first of a series of short spurs of land extends for a short distance to the south before hooking back sharply eastward. Collectively, perhaps in recognition of their historical appearance, they are known as 'the Marrams' but, despite the presence of the word 'Dunes' on the map, there are today none.

Further to the west along the naked spine of shingle, beyond the lonely Watch House (a former coastguard lookout), lies 'the Hood', an area of low, grassed dunes overlying a complex of further lateral ridges. Then, beyond a further strip of bare shingle, lie the 'Long Hills', a group of higher dune outcrops at the base of a long, forked spit known today as 'Yankee Ridge'. Towards the Point's western end, beyond the long and meandering 'Pinchen's Creek', the ridge is topped with a succession of tall mature dunes. Known as the 'Sandhills' or 'Beacon Hills', they stand like a line of battleships.

Within the dunes, behind the main crest, lies a connected series of flat depressions, or 'lows', dune slacks into which the highest tides seep to form temporary shallow lakes. Beyond, invisible until the top of the dunes is reached, lies a short low recurve (now known as 'Near Point'), then a deep bay of thick, sloppy mud and, finally, a long bright dune and a final great accumulation of shingle known simply as 'Far Point'. Beyond lies the Blakeney Channel, the great sandbanks in front of Stiffkey and Warham and the distant blurred line of Holkham Meals.

The shingle backbone, this great linear accumulation of pebbles eight miles long but no more than three hundred metres wide and ten metres high, provides Blakeney Point's basic structure. Although its features can be appreciated at ground level, it is best seen from above, from a map or, better still, from an aerial photograph.

From this angle the eye notices on the seaward side the lean line and then the smooth curve of the outer beach but on its sheltered inland flank the lateral ridges protrude like the clustered broken teeth of a comb and the eye is struck by the delicate threaded labyrinth of the saltmarsh and its winding creeks. From this perspective the Point's whole shape is striking too: a great arm reaching out to the west-northwest, its hand grasping wildly for the Stiffkey shore. The comparison with an outstretched arm and hand is uncannily accurate; forearm, wrist, hand and great clawing fingers are all present, well-defined and in proportion. With a bit of finger-puppetry in front of a lamp, it is easy to make a near-perfect outline of Blakeney Point on the wall.

But in reality the shape of Blakeney Point is not so easily defined. If we compare the landscape before us with its shape on the map we start to notice differences. Most obviously, the River Glaven does not flow as it is marked. Seeking an answer in older maps confounds the problem further. Now the land assumes a different shape and the river has shifted once more. On even older maps the geography is yet more unfamiliar.

By studying these changes it is possible to deduce that the extension of the Point as far west as the village of Cley might date back to only around 1200 AD, at which time the estuary of the River Glaven was broad and faced due north to the open sea. On the first crude map of the area dating from 1586 we see Blakeney Point as a broad protrusion of land extending west to a position just north of Blakeney Church, forcing the river to adopt a more westerly course before turning north once more and reaching the sea between Blakeney and Morston.

By 1693, a chart in *Great Britain's Coasting Pilot* (produced by Captain Greenville Collins for Charles II) shows that the shingle ridge has extended rapidly, its tip now lying just to the west of Morston. A large terminal 'hook' or 'headland' has also developed. On this map the marshes in front of Salthouse, Cley and Blakeney have been reclaimed, enclosed behind sea walls, restricting the eastern extension of the estuary, once extending broadly as far as Kelling, to a narrow channel. Then, in William Faden's map of Norfolk (produced between 1790 and 1794) a further small extension to the Point has occurred and there are now two terminal spits, whilst the shingle ridge has thinned considerably and the whole structure has moved inland around three hundred metres.

Since the nineteenth century more accurate mapping has been carried out by the Ordnance Survey and even more change is laid bare. By 1886 the headland has become a more significant feature, the furthest spit now lying well to the west of Morston. A new far spit has developed but after the storm surge of 1897 it vanishes from the map. Two new terminal spits have formed by 1913 but by 1919 these have fused into a single structure. Even more dramatic change can be seen on the map for 1922: now the River Glaven has been artificially realigned to run through a new channel across Blakeney Freshes. By 1965 the terminal spit has been shortened and now points more to the south but the following year a new terminal spit has started to appear. This new 'Far Point' continues to grow to this day.

We turn instinctively to maps for reassurance, for confirmation in their precise lines and shading that the landscape can be delineated and fixed. But maps, we learn here, are merely an illusion, a construct of the imagination, an expression of our desire for order and precision. These processes of spit formation, reshaping and destruction ensure the imminent redundancy of any published chart. Why, we are forced to reflect, does this place have its own geographical rules? Why does it deny the laws of topographical permanence? Why is it so restless, refusing to be mapped?

Until as recently as the eighteenth century, the received wisdom was that the earth, once created, was permanent and immutable. The shoreline lay where it had always lain, its rocks and dunes holding back the sea and a return of the Flood. For centuries such certainties stifled any further consideration of the issue. Eventually, however, some began to question whether the great features on the earth's surface - the soaring mountain ranges, the boundless oceans and, in particular, the boundary between the two - were really quite so fixed after all.

Some went as far as to argue that the Flood was merely a fable and that the landscape and coastline had been formed not by single creative or destructive events but by a continuous process of interminably slow and relentless change. The leading exponents of this view were two Scottish geologists: James Hutton and Charles Lyell. In Hutton's *Theory of the Earth,* written between 1785 and 1799, and Lyell's *Principles of Geology,* written between 1830 and 1833, can be found a wholly new idea, that the apparent permanence of the earth and its shorelines is an illusion. Instead, these pioneering geologists postulate an endless, infinitely ancient process in which rocks are laid down as deposits on the seabed, uplifted into great mountain ranges, tilted and warped, eroded away, inundated once more and then buried under further deposits.

Today we know that buried a thousand metres below Blakeney Point lies the northern edge of an ancient platform of flat rock known as the Anglo-Brabant Massif. Around 300 million years ago this rock was progressively buried under a layer of sand and, during the Cretaceous period of 144-65 million years ago, gradually inundated by rising seas. Calcareous algae and plankton were abundant in these warm, shallow, subtropical waters, their dead bodies accumulating over many millions of years to form a thick layer of chalk. Within this layer could also be found concentrations of silica from the exoskeletons of dead sponge-like creatures. Over millions of years these would harden to become the flint nodules we see today. Thus was formed the Point's underlying structure, what is known by geologists as its 'bedrock geology'.

Then, about sixty-five million years ago, the Yucatan meteor strike ushered in a new geological era: the Pleistocene. This was characterised by a profound cooling, a rereat of the sea (which exposed north Norfolk's chalk platform) and, above all, by a succession of glaciations. Though their influence was brief in geological terms, the ice had a dramatic effect on the landscape. It is entirely responsible for what geologists call the 'superficial geology', the surface features we see today.

Our understandings of these processes are also recent. In 1840 the Swiss scientist Louis Agassiz proposed in *Etudes sur les Glaciers* the shocking notion of an 'Ice Age'. The northern lands (including Europe), he argued, had once been covered by a great thickness of ice. A great ice wall had ground its way south, crushing, scraping and reshaping the landscape as it went and pushing before it vast quantities of rock, gravel and glacial debris. More shocking still was the assertion that this had happened in the relatively recent past, perhaps as little as twelve thousand years ago. The evidence for this, argued Agassiz, lay all around in the erratic rocks, glacial till and sculpted valleys of northern and central Europe. This was a horrifying and apocalyptic theory but one which, given the abundant evidence to hand, was hard to dismiss.

There is continuing debate about the precise calendar of ice advances but there is general agreement that around 300,000 years ago the first of these great gouging glaciers, the Anglian, ground its way south, colliding with the chalk platform to create a great terminal moraine, an enormous accumulation of glacial material, across what is now north Norfolk. Here lie the origins of the area's physical features, most notably the Holt-Cromer ridge, the line of high ground visible from Blakeney Point to the southeast. Then came further glacial advances, first, around 200,000 years ago, the Wolstonian ice and then, around 110,000 years ago, that of the Devensian.

Around twelve thousand years ago, at the beginning of the Holocene era, temperatures began to rise once more and the great buttresses of ice began to retreat. As they disappeared they left behind a scoured, scraped land, dotted with bright lakes and strewn with glacial moraines and debris: boulder clay, sand and gravel. With the final retreat of the Devensian ice came, as in each of the previous interglacial periods, further dramatic landscape change. As the glaciers melted, huge amounts of freshwater augmented the oceans, leading to dramatic sea level rise and further great movements of the earth's shorelines.

However, this was no steady, uniform process. The last twelve thousand years have seen a succession of warm periods interspersed with returns to near-glacial conditions, the coastline shifting to and fro in tune with this oscillation. There have been other factors at work too. As the immense crushing weight of the ice retreated, the process of 'isostatic rebound' caused northern Britain to rise but southern England to sink in compensation, exacerbating sea level rise in East Anglia and further reshaping the coast.

Finally the rising sea flooded the extensive marshy lowlands which connected eastern England with the rest of the continent and then, around seven thousand years ago, the waters overran what are now the Straits of Dover, severing Britain's link with Europe. By around four thousand years ago the shoreline was close to its present position. This, however, did not signify a new period of stability. The last four thousand years have seen a continuous process of coastal change, of movement, accretion and erosion.

Today the study of the evolution and configuration of coastal landforms, this most recent manifestation of an infinitely old process, has come to be known as 'coastal geomorphology', a brand new area of scientific study. Building on the work of geologists, this discipline deals not with the hard rocks which here are buried beneath the surface but with the softer surface geology and its interaction with the sea.

In this context Blakeney Point demonstrates a whole array of shaping forces: sea level fluctuations, offshore currents, sediment movement, wind, wave action, tides and human impacts. Not without reason is it widely recognised as a classic case study, extensively researched and internationally famous, amongst those places most cited in physical geography textbooks and now officially listed as of prime scientific importance.

In the early years of the twentieth century, however, the study of coastal geography was a young science. Amongst its earliest exponents was the American Douglas Wilson Johnson. His *Shore Processes and Shoreline Development*, published in 1919, was the first to attempt a classification of coastal types and was for a time the most influential work on the subject. In England a comprehensive review of the coastal landscape was undertaken by Edith Marjorie Ward in her 1922 *English Coastal Evolution*. Here an attempt is made to understand the processes of offshore bar formation in north Norfolk, particularly at Blakeney Point. Although this is a somewhat cursory treatment, the significance of the Point in the study of coastal geography had nevertheless been recognised. The subject had also been addressed, at least in part, by Francis Oliver and Edward Salisbury in their 1913 'Blakeney Point, Norfolk: Topography and Vegetation' and again by Oliver in his 1918 *Tidal Lands: a study of shore problems*, a collaboration with the civil engineer Alfred E. Carey in which a whole chapter is devoted to Blakeney Point and the role of vegetation in sea defences.

Oliver and Salisbury were, of course, botanists and ecologists, not physical geographers. Their interest in the Point's physical features was focused more on their role in hosting plant communities than on their nature and origin. However, the coast of north Norfolk, and Blakeney Point in particular, was soon to be thrust centre-stage in this new science. The man responsible for establishing the study of the coast as a fully-fledged discipline, and ultimately for Blakeney Point's renown amongst coastal geographers, was James Alfred Steers. One of a new generation of geologists at St. Catharine's College, Cambridge in the years after the First War, Steers became Professor of Geography there in 1949 until his retirement in 1966. During his time at St. Catharine's he built Cambridge into a leading centre in the study of physical geography and also made a lasting contribution to post-war planning, arguing for the protection of the coastline from damaging development.

Steers was keenly aware of the need for geography to connect with other disciplines, most notably geology and ecology. Geologists interpret the ancient processes which have produced today's coast while botanists and ecologists study the interaction of vegetation with changing coastal landforms. The boundaries of the coastal geographer's work are therefore not clearly defined. Steers was quick to recognise such inter-dependencies and argue for collaborative, multi-disciplinary approaches amongst scientists:

> Perhaps one of the most significant lessons that has been learned is the value of multi-disciplinary work; a far better understanding of natural phenomena is likely to result from collaborative investigations in the field by specialists in different subjects.

Such collaboration was warmly welcomed by Oliver. Blakeney Point was, he argued, 'the kindergarten of all shore study' and Steers was 'the first man who has ever come to take advantage of the very evident facilities which such spots afford'. Steers's arrival was, for Oliver 'an event in the history of Blakeney Point'.

Although Steers was involved in research work as far afield as Australia and Jamaica, and familiar with the whole coastline of England and Wales (and much of Scotland), it is for his work in north Norfolk, notably at Scolt Head Island and Blakeney Point, that he is best known. This coastline was his greatest love and, through its study, he became the leading figure in this new science.

Steers published widely during his career. His first paper, 'The East Anglian Coast', was published in *The Geographical Journal* in 1927 and was followed in 1934 by his celebrated work *Scolt Head Island*. He went on to publish a long list of books on the British coast, most notably *The Coastline of England and Wales* in 1946. Here he admits that:

> I have... found it far more difficult to write about cliffed coasts than flat coasts. Whereas in the latter there is often an interesting

physiographical evolution to trace, and also a relationship between physical features, history and archaeology, in describing the former it is hard to avoid a dull statement of rather obvious facts.

Perhaps his best known work is his 1953 book *The Sea Coast,* a volume in the popular (and highly collectable) 'New Naturalist' series.

In all these publications Steers sets out his theories on beach formation and movement and on the origins and development of shingle spits, dunes and saltmarshes. In respect of the former he examines the well-known examples of Orford Ness, Dungeness, Chesil Beach and Slapton Ley but, due to its combination of all three habitat types, it is Blakeney Point which features most prominently.

Here, he argues, fine material such as mud and sand has been brought by sea currents. North Norfolk, he suggests, acts like a great east-west groyne, capturing sediment drifting south from the crumbling and fast-eroding clay cliffs of Holderness. The north coast, he proposes, also receives material from the east, from the erosion of the cliffs between Weybourne Hope and Sheringham.

At the base of these soft cliffs the underlying chalk platform studded with flints is exposed. Above lies a deep layer of sand, gravel and clay. These cliffs are under constant attack. In periods of heavy rain, great 'slumps' of waterlogged clay slide down the cliffs whilst the sea constantly nibbles away at the chalk base. In storms and heavy seas this process is, of course, much accelerated. Some of the resulting fine material is then carried east and then south around the East Anglian coast, but Sheringham marks an important divide. West of here, the movement is to the west, to Blakeney Point and beyond.

Steers's key argument, however, is that the role of currents is limited. Currents may move mud and sand but they are too weak to shift larger material and they are, of course, only capable of moving material which is actually in the water. Material on the beach itself cannot be affected by currents. Steers proposes that it is wave action, not currents, which has created and shaped the characteristic features of the north Norfolk coast. Blakeney Point, he argues, was built from offshore sea gravels, glacial residues, swept onshore by wave action as Holocene sea levels rose and the shoreline advanced south. Today's ridge is no longer accumulating new shingle but it is still subjected to considerable movement and reshaping by the waves.

This wave action is, of course, a function of the wind, with the energy which waves release on the shore being determined by the strength of the wind and the distance over which the wave has travelled. The greater the 'fetch' - the length of unimpeded journey - the greater the height and power of the waves. Winds of local origin produce small, irregular waves but those from a longer distance are both larger and more regular. The power of the breaking wave moves shingle up the beach but because the backwash is much weaker most of the shingle remains there, along the ridge's crown, unaffected by all but the highest tides. Blakeney Point is therefore a prime example of a 'constructive' beach, one to which material is added or accreted. On 'destructive' beaches the opposite applies and considerable erosion occurs.

However, the shingle is not only moved up the beach. It is also moved sideways, thereby causing the relentless westward movement and growth of the spit. The lateral movement of the shingle can be seen, suggests Steers, by watching a breaking wave. If it strikes at an oblique angle it drives small stones up the beach at the same angle, only for the stones to roll down the slope at ninety degrees to the beach as the wave retreats. The result of thousands of such wave movements is that the whole beach moves slowly back and forth. Though the *prevalent* wind direction at Blakeney Point is from the west and southwest, the greater fetch of winds from the northeast ensures that, over time, more material is moved to the west. The northeast wind is therefore *dominant* and, over time, moves the most shingle.

There is a particular tension at Blakeney Point due to its near east-west orientation for here the prevalent and dominant winds oppose each other. A constant battle betwen these two forces therefore ensues and the process of beach movement, or 'beach drift', is erratic. When westerly and southwesterly winds are at their most prevalent and the advance of the shingle is checked, wave action bends the tip of the ridge back to form a hook but with the increasing frequency of northeasterly winds the shingle continues its inexorable march to the west, interrupting the process of hook formation, cutting off its supply of material and marooning it in a state of permanently arrested development. It now becomes the latest in the series of lateral recurves, with a new, and of course itself also temporary, terminal spit then created to the west. Sometimes these new spits are formed in rapid succession and so occur close together (most notably in the Marrams) but at other times (such as between the Watch House and the Hood and between the Hood and the Long Hills) the sea's energies are devoted for longer periods to the westward extension of the ridge.

Steers cautions, therefore, that old maps need to be interpreted with care. They may be inaccurate and they may also lead the geographer into assuming an even rate of beach movement. The reality may, of course, be much more complex, with periods of slower or more rapid movement perhaps even punctuated by reverses of direction. He asks, for example, whether the Point was always attached to the mainland at its eastern end or whether it might have been an offshore bar formed in the same manner as Scolt Head which was then 'captured' by a westward-growing spit from Weybourne.

With the establishment of a firm and relatively stable shingle base, Steers goes on to describe the next stage in the Point's development: the growth of dunes. If the shingle ridge can be seen as the Point's 'spine' or 'skeleton', then its dunes form part of its 'flesh'. The dunes are a product of the wind and the interaction of sand and vegetation. Blown by the prevailing winds from the extensive foreshore to the west, sand begins to accrete around any small object. Low sand ridges then begin to rise, slowly growing in height and spreading sideways, joining up with others and finally forming dunes. Integral to the process is colonisation by dune-building grasses which bind the sand together with their long root systems. The process continues until the onward march of the ridge and the formation of a new terminal spit cuts the dune off from its supply of wind-blown sand and the process starts again further to the west.

As with the beach, though, the dunes are not static features. Depite the illusion of permanence they too are drifting across the landscape, rising and maturing before disintegrating and disappearing. Any small gap or tear in the vegetation cover, caused by the wind, Rabbits or human trampling, can give the wind leverage to create a 'blowout' which can then grow to form a great scar or hole in the dune or, in extreme cases, destroy it altogether. For example, the old Long Hills, the line of dunes along Yankee Ridge, clearly marked on old maps, are long gone whilst new fore-dunes continue to accrete along the Point's outer fringe.

The final process described by Steers is the growth of the saltmarsh. In this respect, Blakeney Point provides a near-perfect example of its development behind an offshore bar. As the shingle extends westward and throws out its hooks to the south it slowly encloses an ever greater area, protecting it from the direct attack of the sea. Here, on the Point's inland flank, the great shaping force is the tide. On the steeply-shelving outer beach the sea rises and falls in a twice-daily rhythm - a frontal assault by crashing waves - but on the inland side it crawls across a flat landscape of intertidal mud and sand, its advance more clandestine, more secretive, a steady stalking and encirclement from the rear.

Here the estuary floor is not uniform and any slight ripple or irregularity in the sand is sufficient to trap silt carried down into the Harbour by the Glaven and the Stiffkey, particularly where the water is shallow and calm. Most of this deposition is likely to occur during the slack period around high water and it is likely to be greatest in the still and sheltered conditions between the laterals. Over time this process, much like that which creates the dunes, forms higher and longer features which join together and become more substantial. At the same time, drainage channels develop between them which, over time, evolve into an embryonic creek system.

The process of saltmarsh formation then proceeds through the progressive colonisation of saltmarsh plants. These in turn increase the rate of deposition and the new saltmarsh both rises vertically and expands horizontally. With increasing height comes less frequent immersion and new niches for plants to colonise. Eventually the mature saltmarsh is covered in a mat of thick vegetation and, as it continues to rise, it further defines and deepens the creeks.

All these processes - the movement of sand and shingle, the growth of dunes and the development of saltmarshes - are the result of tiny, incremental changes. However, much more sudden and dramatic change can come to this coast.

Steers published *Coast and Sea* in 1953, a year which was to bring this interplay of land and sea to a much wider audience than a few coastal geographers. Indeed so signifcant were the events of that year that Steers was moved to describe them in a last-minute Appendix to his book.

On 30th January 1953 the nation's attention was focused on events at sea in the North Channel, between southern Scotland and Northern Ireland. MV *Princess Victoria*, bound for Larne from Stranraer, foundered in rough seas and sank with the loss of 133 lives. This tragedy was just the prelude, however, the opening act to an even greater tragedy stalking in the wings.

On the morning of 30th the area of low pressure responsible for these severe conditions lay south of Iceland. It deepened rapidly as it continued east during the day and by 6 p.m. it was located near the Faeroes with its central pressure down to 980 mb and increasingly strong northerly winds around its rear edge. By midday on 31st, now with a central pressure of only 968 mb, it moved into the northern North Sea. Now the storm's greatest force was transferred to the east coast where it became more violent still, briefly reaching hurricane-force. For a short while this was the worst northerly gale on record.

The low atmospheric pressure had the effect of raising the sea's surface, producing a great 'hump' of water. Combined with the storm-force wind, this pushed a great surge south down the North Sea. As it did so, it found itself constricted by ever-narrowing coastlines and by an ever-rising sea-floor, forcing the water to rise up higher and higher. As it travelled down the English east coast it also coincided with a high tide period. The combination of storm surge, high tide and violent wave action would bring catastrophe.

As darkness fell on 31st the great wall of water hit Lincolnshire before meeting the north Norfolk coast head-on. Although high tide was due at 8 p.m., by 5 p.m. the water was already dangerously high. With three hours of tide still to run, a disaster was unavoidable and, by the time of high water, sea levels were over two metres higher than predicted.

At Blakeney Point it is normal for the highest tides to overrun the saltmarsh, flood the belts of Suaeda bushes, encircle the dunes, cut off the outermost spits and seep into the lows. At such times the main shingle ridge is constricted to a narrow spine, the Point almost an island. Now, however, the main shingle ridge itself was overrun, with only the high dunes remaining above water. The Watch House was seriously flooded and water was five feet deep in the old Lifeboat House. Along the whole length of the main ridge the shingle was pushed over the top of the bank and rolled down the lee side, burying the Suaeda, piling up against it or protruding through gaps in great three-foot high 'fans' reaching out onto the saltmarsh. The shingle also tumbled into the channel of the River Glaven, constricting and threatening to block its flow, whilst great slices were taken off the front of the dunes. In all, the whole ridge lurched suddenly inland by around fifty metres.

At Blakeney Point the surge merely reshaped the landscape. Elsewhere, however, the damage was more serious. At Wells, Blakeney, Cley and Salthouse the sea walls were breached, deep water flowed into the villages and, in an echo of former times, the River Glaven was inundated as far upstream as Glandford.

Further afield - in east Norfolk, in Suffolk, Essex and north Kent - it was even worse. Altogether, 24,000 homes were damaged and over three hundred lives were lost. In the Netherlands the consequences were even more severe.

The severity of the 1953 surge was exceptional but such events are not unprecedented. Many others are documented in the historical record, that of 18th November 1897 being particularly severe. A contemporary eye-witness describes the scene at Cley:

> Between eight o'clock and noon the crests of the breakers were visible to an unusual extent above the ridge of the sea-wall. Presently a rent was made, speedily to be followed by others, and mighty waves coursed inland, filling the dykes and flooding the marshes.

Since 1953 other surges have occurred: on 11th January 1978, 19th-20th February 1996 and 9th November 2007. Though all were damaging, and all rolled the shingle inland once more, none was as severe as that of 1953.

1953 was a 'wake-up call', a timely reminder that the study of the coast is no mere academic exercise. The interplay of land and sea is not purely of interest to geographers; it has real consequences for anyone living near the sea. Today, over fifty years after Steers's pioneering work, coastal change is even higher on our agenda. Not only do we have to plan for the inevitable repetition of the events of 1953 but we also have to consider further sea level rise and potentially even more rapid coastal change. In 2002 the River Glaven had to be re-routed once more and even more significant changes to the coast are envisaged in today's 'Shoreline Management Plan'.

But this coast brings more than physical challenges. It also challenges our notions of permanency and place. One of the things we take most for granted is the constancy of the earth underfoot. We talk of the hard materiality of the world, of the 'solid earth', of 'solid ground' beneath our feet and conceive of it as a place fixed in space and time, a place we can describe and define, a place we can revisit, where our footsteps can be retraced and where our memories are preserved.

At Blakeney Point, however, these notions are turned on their head. Here we see not a stable, permanent scene but a dynamic landscape. Every day the sea builds up its shingle and rearranges it but it also seeks to overrun and destroy it. Blakeney Point exists in a state of permanent tension, at the mercy of the forces of accretion and erosion, on the front line of the age-old battle between land and sea. It is not a line on a map. It is tranisent, mobile, ever-changing, built up, worn down, moved around and reshaped. This is the earth at its most capricious and disorientating, a place where everything shifts and nothing is certain.

6

DOWN THE LONG WIND

*And fainter onward, like wild birds that change
Their season in the night and wail their way
From cloud to cloud, down the long wind…*

Alfred Lord Tennyson

In the post-war period Blakeney Point found itself at the forefront of another new concept: that of the bird observatory, a place for the systematic observation and trapping of migrant birds and the correlation of these studies with the weather conditions. These ideas had first developed elsewhere but the eventual establishment of a bird observatory on the Point yielded a wealth of new facts about bird migration. However, the bird observatories were as important for the experiences they offered as they were for the knowledge they generated. Their work tapped into man's age-old fascination with the migrations of birds, providing a front-row seat for some exceptional avian drama and inspiring a whole new generation of birdwatchers.

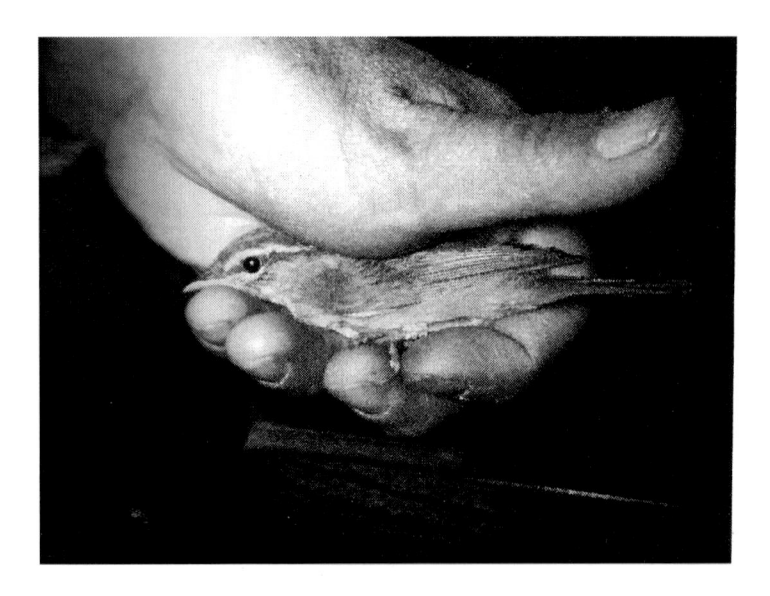

Plate 11. The 1961 Radde's Warbler (*Cley Bird Observatory*)

Plate 12. Richard Richardson at the Hood (*Cley Bird Observatory*)

Autumn comes quickly to Blakeney Point. By October the mornings are already colder and the surf crashes more heavily on the beach. Inland, colour blazes in the fields and copses but here it seeps away, leaving a landscape of spare, austere tones. Now the dune-top grasses bend before the wind and the sand hisses along the beach, mingling with the sea's more urgent roar.

This is the time of year when the migrant birds come, fleeing from the advancing cold and dwindling food of their northern homes. With an east wind the drab Suaeda bushes are full of tired and hungry Robins and Goldcrests, fresh in from their crossing of the North Sea. Also arriving are other fellow travellers from Scandinavia and Russia - Redwings, Fieldfares and Blackbirds - all seeking food and rest before resuming their search for a winter home.

Throughout history we have been inspired by the mysterious appearance of migratory birds. Theirs is, of course, just one of many migrations - mammals, fish, butterflies and many other creatures undertake predictable seasonal movements - but that of birds has most consistently captured the human imagination. Their arrivals and departures mark the year's rhythms but understanding their movements has always proved difficult.

Aristotle recognised that some birds, such as Cranes, migrated over large distances but he also believed that others, including Swallows, hibernated at the bottom of ponds. This latter theory was still widely, though not universally, upheld even into the eighteenth century. The Willughby and Ray *Ornithologia* of 1676 says of migrant birds that 'To us it seems more probable that they fly away into hot countries, viz. Egypt, Ethiopia etc.' but over a century later Gilbert White's *The Natural History of Selborne* contains further arguments in favour of hibernation, at least by a few species:

> At least many of the swallow kind do not leave us in the winter, but lay themselves up like insects and bats, in a torpid state, to slumber away the more uncomfortable months till the return of the sun and fine weather awakens them.

Even though migration has long fascinated the human mind, our understandings of the phenomenon are still far from complete. The systematic study of bird migration is only just over a hundred years old but in this time it has become one of ornithology's chief preoccupations.

We know that birds migrate for the simple reason that the earth's north/south axis is tilted at an angle of 23.4 degrees to the vertical. Each winter brings a 'mini Ice Age' to the northern hemisphere but as the Pole swings back towards the sun, light and warmth flood north, triggering a great flowering of plants and a new abundance of insects. To exploit this bounty comes first a slow trickle and then a great tide of birds. As autumn comes, the Pole swings away from the sun once more, propelling a whole new generation of birds to the south.

We know much less, however, about how these great feats of travel and endurance are achieved. Many mechanisms have been implicated - navigation by the sun and stars, genetic inheritance, magnetic compass, sound echoes, differences in air pressure - but the true mix is still not understood. We still do not know how birds go to places they have never seen or how they know when they have arrived. Most of our knowledge of bird migration remains at the more basic level of recording what we see.

Much of this knowledge was, of course, gained from the activities of the nineteenth century collectors, notably at Blakeney Point. In the course of their pursuits, new species were discovered to be reaching Britain and the occurrence patterns of our migrant birds became much more clearly understood but, for all their protestations of scientific endeavour, theirs was ultimately a chase, a quest for prestige and financial gain in which the gathering of scientific knowledge was largely incidental.

Others, however, were taking more of a scientific interest in migration and its mysteries, though the collection of specimens remained, for a while, an important part of this research. The key figure in defining this new kind of study was a German, Heinrich Gätke. Originally a marine painter, in 1837 he moved to the tiny island of Heligoland, off Germany's northwest coast. Here he was captivated by what he describes as 'that strange and mysterious phenomenon in the life of birds, their migratory journeys' which has 'for thousands of years called forth the astonishment and admiration of mankind'.

He was to remain on the island for some fifty years, constantly acquiring specimens but also taking notes on all the birds which came his way. Heligoland, it quickly became clear, was an outstanding place for this type of study, providing both large numbers of birds and the previously unsuspected but in fact regular and predictable occurrence of rarities.

Gätke was not a trained scientist but he was an enthusiastic and astute observer, recording not just the birds but the patterns formed by their occurrences: the orderly progress of migration according to the season, the direction of migration, its altitude and velocity and the influence of weather. Gätke discovered for himself many of the phenomena familiar to migration students today. For example, he observed a great difference in the character of the two migration seasons, noting that the mix of species at each is not the same. He also noted that most migration takes place at night and that much of it passes high overhead, only becoming visible on the ground when weather conditions are adverse. He realised too that most passage occurs on a broad front, a view not shared by the contemporary ornithological establishment which believed in narrow 'flyways'.

Amongst his other insights was the observation that migrants in spring have a strong northeastward component to their movements whereas in autumn the dominant direction of passage is to the southwest. He also understood that each species has its own particular 'slot' in the migration calendar and that its appearance or absence at this time is determined entirely by the weather.

Gätke acquired a particularly keen understanding of this aspect of migration:

> We have already laid stress on the fact that such portions of the migration phenomenon as become apparent during its periodical recurrences, are brought within the range of our observing faculties almost exclusively by meteorological conditions which are exercising a disturbing influence upon the normal progress of the migratory movement.

He understood that in autumn a drop in temperature and winds from the east or northeast could produce large arrivals of birds whereas mild winds from the west or southwest would produce very few. In spring, however, the most favourable winds for bird arrivals were warm light breezes from the south and southeast.

Gätke was very familiar with that greatest of all prizes for the British collector: the Bluethroat. He notes of the species:

> One would hardly believe that the home of so lovely a creature as the Bluethroat extended so far north as the coast of the Polar Sea, particularly as its beautiful azure blue and rusty orange dress gives one the impresion of its being a native of tropical latitudes.

Long before the Power brothers discovered the Bluethroats of Blakeney Point, Gätke was observing them on Heligoland. Here it was 'of quite common and generally known occurrence', a regular migrant in both spring and autumn. In the spring Gätke notes that southeast winds can produce large numbers and that he has on such occasions obtained as many as fifty males in the course of a day. In autumn it is described as being even commoner, with sometimes hundreds of birds frequenting the potato fields. Gätke was well aware of its rarity in Britain, however, concluding correctly that Heligoland lay at the western edge of the species' migration route.

Gätke also made other discoveries, most notably the occurrence of Siberian birds whose normal wintering grounds lie in Southeast Asia. The two most regularly occurring were Yellow-browed Warbler and Richard's Pipit, both species whose breeding range lies far to the east, beyond the Urals. Gätke noted at least eighty of the former and many hundreds of the latter, despite their being barely recorded anywhere else in Europe at the time.

He also realised the importance of the calendar and the weather in these arrivals, noting that they only appeared on predictable dates (in late September and October) and that they only did so in years which saw easterly winds at this time. Indeed his correspondence with Russian meteorologists confirmed that those years which saw the greatest influxes of these rarities were those in which the easterly airflow extended most deeply into Russia. So regular and predictable were these arrivals, argued Gätke, that they constituted not the random, accidental movements of lost birds but deliberate migrations by a small part of the population.

Gätke was, however, somewhat prone to speculation, and some of his ideas on migration have proved to be flawed. His assertions that birds could fly as high as 40,000 feet and at speeds of up to 180 miles per hour were wildly over-optimistic but although some of his musings have turned out to be misguided, the reliability of his actual observations has been repeatedly confirmed.

Gätke wrote up his whole life's work in his 1895 *The Birds of Heligoland* or *Heligoland as an Ornithological Observatory*. Here, in the word 'observatory' ('vogelwarte' in the original German) was expressed for the first time a wholly new idea, the prospectus, in effect, for a wholly new kind of study: that of long term systematic observations at a single, favoured site.

It was not long before these ideas were taken up in Britain, a process assisted by Gätke's contact with two British ornithologists. The first of these was John Cordeaux of Great Coates in north Lincolnshire, a stone's throw from the Humber estuary and an ideal location for the study of migration. Cordeaux's first written contribution on the subject was a paper in *The Zoologist* of April 1864 concerning a large influx of Goldcrests on the east coast the previous October. Most inspiring to Cordeaux, however, was his visit to Heligoland in September 1874 where he met Gätke, and thereafter the two men were regular correspondents, reporting on their respective sightings. Soon Cordeaux was making similar observations, noting in one of his letters to his German friend:

> On that portion of the east coast of England which lies opposite Heligoland, birds are in the habit of appearing in large numbers with easterly and southeasterly winds, but that, with winds in the opposite direction their numbers observed are very small.

Cordeaux began an enquiry into migration patterns on the east coast in the autumn of 1876, approaching lighthouse and lightship keepers for their observations. The results were published in *The Zoologist* in January 1877. A wider survey was undertaken in 1879 with the Scottish ornithologist John Harvie-Brown, with reporting forms issued to over a hundred lighthouses and lightships around Scotland and England's east coast. Their report was published in *The Zoologist* in May 1880, leading to a series of even more extensive surveys, covering the entire British coastline, between 1880 and 1887, overseen by the Migration Committee of the British Association for the Advancement of Science.

Gätke's other important British contact was the Sheffield steel manufacturer and ornithologist Henry Seebohm. After the first of Seebohm's pioneering expeditions to the Russian Arctic (which he had undertaken in 1875 with Harvie-Brown), Gätke had invited him to Heligoland. Seebohm visited in 1876 and spent nearly a month on the island at the height of the autumn migration season. Writing of his experiences in a chapter of his 1880 *Siberia in Europe: A Visit to the Valley of the Petchora, in North-east Russia*, he records that:

> Mr. Gätke... invited me to visit the island, to renew the acquaintance of the grey plover, the little stint, the bluethroat, the shore lark, the little bunting, and others of my Petchora friends, and to see something of the wonderful stream of migration which sets in every autumn from the Arctic region to the sunny South, and flows abundantly past the island.

Seebohm was impressed with both the number and variety of migrant birds, noting with enthusiasm that 'your next shot may be a corncrake, followed by a ring ousel or a Richard's pipit'. He was also impressed with Gätke's local knowledge. For days Heligoland experienced strong westerly winds, causing Seebohm to remark that 'sometimes for a week together you may diligently tramp the potatoes without finding a bird'. Eventually, though, the wind dropped and swung into the southeast and, exactly as predicted by Gätke, a large arrival of birds took place, including a Yellow-browed Warbler in his garden which fell to Seebohm's gun. 'Migration', observed Seebohm, 'is a question of wind and weather'.

Soon, the British interest in migration study extended beyond correspondence with and trips to Heligoland. The race was now on to find comparable locations on our own shores. Chief amongst the next generation of migration students was William Eagle Clarke, Keeper of the Natural History Department at the Royal Scottish Museum. Eagle Clarke had counted Cordeaux as one of his 'most intimate' friends so was well aware of his pioneering work with lighthouses and lightships.

He visited the Eddystone lighthouse in the autumn of 1901 and the Kentish Knock lightship in 1903, recording many migrant birds including, at the latter, a Richard's Pipit. He later went on to pioneer a number of remote island outposts including Sule Skerry, the Flannan Isles, Ushant, St. Kilda and, most importantly, Fair Isle. He was to visit this tiny island between

Orkney and Shetland many times, annually in the autumns of 1905 to 1909 and then in the springs of 1909 to 1911, by which time he was engaging the help of local observers to continue his work at other times of year. Fair Isle proved to be an outstanding migration site and, with much justification, he was able to declare it to be 'the British Heligoland'.

Like Gätke in Germany, Eagle Clarke went on to make many important discoveries about the nature, extent and timing of migration and also began to rewrite the British status of a number of previous great rarities. In particular, some of the species recorded on Heligoland were found to be regular visitors here also, findings which, of course, also reflected the discoveries made by the gentlemen gunners of Blakeney Point. The Bluethroat, for example, was regular on Fair Isle in small numbers in both spring and autumn, the Yellow-browed Warbler was an annual visitor, with up to seven recorded in a day, and a number of Richard's Pipits were also seen. These and many other of Eagle Clarke's discoveries are documented in his *Studies in Bird Migration*, published in 1912.

Other Scots were also leading the way in migration studies. From 1907 to 1933 the 'Good Ladies' Evelyn Vida Baxter and Leonora Jeffrey Rintoul pioneered the ornithological possibilities of the Isle of May, in the outer reaches of the Firth of Forth. Here they recorded many migrant birds and, as at Fair Isle, they also demonstrated the occurrence of rarities.

It was the Germans who established the first permanent bird observatories - in 1901 at Rossitten on the Baltic shore of East Prussia (now Rybachi in Russia's Kaliningrad Oblast) and, in 1909, on Heligoland - but in 1927 Ronald Lockley took up residence on the Pembrokeshire island of Skokholm and added the study of migrant birds to that of the island's seabirds. A 'Heligoland trap' (a large wire mesh frame tapering to a small catching box) was built and Skokholm was recognised as Britain's first bird observatory in 1933. Inspired by this development and by the ground-breaking work of Baxter and

Rintoul, the Isle of May became Britain's second observatory in 1934.

The Second War soon intervened but its end ushered in a new era of enthusiasm for migration study. In quick succession other bird observatories were established at Yorkshire's Spurn Point, at Lundy in the Bristol Channel, at Lincolnshire's Gibraltar Point and, of course, on Fair Isle. It was here that perhaps the last migrant bird was shot by an ornithologist. In October 1952, after some debate over the identity of a small lark, Colonel Richard Meinertzhagen produced a shotgun, secured it and pronounced it to be a Short-toed Lark, to the considerable consternation of his companions.

A new Bird Observatories Committee was soon formed and a working definition of a bird observatory agreed. It was to be 'a field station cooperatively manned for the purpose of making continuous observations on migrant birds and for catching, examining and marking them'.

This latter aspect was to be an important function. The marking of birds dates back to Roman times but the first recognisably modern bird ringing scheme using lightweight aluminium rings identified by a unique serial number and return address was introduced in 1898 by the Dane Hans Christian Cornelius Mortensen. Ringing was also soon carried out at both Rossitten and Heligoland but in 1909 two separate schemes were introduced in Britain, the first by Arthur Landsborough Thomson at Aberdeen University, the other by the great architect of twentieth century ornithology Harry Witherby, in conjunction with his journal *British Birds*. This latter scheme would become the official British scheme after the First War until it was transferred to the care of the Britsh Trust for Ornithology in 1937. As well as generating recoveries, trapping had other important functions too. It provided the opportunity to gather data on racial variation, moult, weight and measurements. There was also much to learn about the identification of rarities.

At Blakeney Point, however, these early developments passed by largely unnoticed. Before the Second War only the occasional visitor noted the comings and goings of birds here, though amongst them was the author Henry Williamson:

> Many birds were arriving from across the sea. They came in twos and threes, and in little flights of straggling flocks. All of them flew a few feet above the waves. They were tired, some were exhausted... I watched the golden-crested wren... come like a hesitant bumble bee and drop into the sandhills, its needle-beak gaping with thirst, its wings drooping with fatigue. Three yellow-grey owls, with short feather tufts like stub-horns on their heads, flapped down soon afterwards.

As the heyday of the gentlemen gunners passed, there was little further enquiry into Blakeney Point's migrant birds. Bob Pinchen and his successors as Watcher Bill and then his son Ted Eales noted birds in the course of their duties but there was nothing resembling the systematic observation and recording of small migrants which was starting to take place elsewhere.

However, Blakeney Point's terns were amongst the very first birds to be ringed anywhere in Britain. This was carried out sporadically between 1909 and 1939, initially by Emma Louisa Turner, the pioneering ornithologist, bird photographer and first Watcher at Scolt Head Island. Ringing the Point's terns yielded valuable recoveries which helped to pinpoint the birds' wintering areas. Both Common and Sandwich Tern chicks were ringed and were subsequently recovered in Angola, Senegal and the Ivory Coast.

After the war, however, Blakeney Point finally caught up with events and quickly found itself in the vanguard of the new bird observatory movement. The key to this transformation was the arrival in Cley in 1949 of a new and inspirational force in the shape of Richard Richardson. An experienced birdwatcher and gifted artist, he was to become perhaps most widely known for illustrating *The Pocket Guide to British Birds*, produced with Richard Fitter and published in 1952.

Richardson was also an enthusiastic ringer and, fully aware of the area's reputation for migrants, he moved quickly to establish

Cley as the country's sixth recognised bird observatory. Its first home was a collection of derelict military buildings behind Cley beach where the accommodation was, to say the least, basic. Here a Heligoland trap was built, its first capture being a Goldcrest.

The observatory was quick to make an impact, documenting in 1951 not only England's first ever Subalpine Warbler but also its share of a memorable October 'rush' of Robins and other migrants (including a handful of Bluethroats on the Point). At first its area of operation was restricted to Cley, to the area between the Cley channel in the west and Walsey Hills on the Salthouse boundary in the east. However, the catastrophic storm surge of 31st January 1953 rewrote the observatory's story overnight. The buildings were severely damaged and the trap destroyed. It was now time for a move to Blakeney Point.

The National Trust gave permission for ringing operations to be carried out here and a hut and double-entrance Heligoland trap were duly constructed at the Hood. Both were in use by the spring of 1954 and accommodation suitable for two 'men students' was made available to visiting ringers at a cost of four shillings a day. Over time the trap was supplemented by the use of other equipment including a portable funnel net, meal-baited spring nets and, from 1956, the newly-invented Japanese mist nets. The observatory's trapping area was small, comprising the area bounded by the outer limits of the Suaeda bushes on the Hood and the crown of the shingle ridge, but nevertheless there was some early success.

On 1st June 1954 a small Robin-like bird was glimpsed as it darted between the Suaeda bushes of the Hood. Another glimpse showed the tell-tale orange patches at either side of the tail. Finally, the bird's identity was fully revealed. It was a Bluethroat, but not the familiar drab bird of autumn. This was a shining bright blue-throated male, the first of its kind ever seen on Blakeney Point in the spring. Next day the bird was still present but it was not shot. Instead it was captured, ringed and carefully measured and weighed before being released unharmed back into the bushes. It was also photographed and its engaging portrait alongside a copy of the relevant volume of Witherby's *Handbook of British Birds* was published in the 1954 *Norfolk Bird Report*.

This Bluethroat could not have been a better omen for ringing operations on the Point. In a neat echo of the Powers' discovery of 1884, it set Cley Bird Observatory on a bold, new course. If nothing else, it proved for the first time that the spring, a season entirely neglected by the gentlemen collectors, was also capable of producing migrant birds and interesting rarities. The early promise of the Hood operations was further reinforced by the capture of both Barred and Aquatic Warblers in August of the same year. So impressed was Richardson with these results that he was to claim, somewhat optimistically, in the *Norfolk Bird Report* that 'the possibilities of the Observatory should approach those of Fair Isle'.

1955 saw the capture of an Icterine Warbler and also England's second Subalpine Warbler, following the first, behind Cley beach, in 1951. Bluethroats proved to be of still regular occurrence in autumn too. These remained a particular favourite and Richardson wrote eloquently of 'the spry and elusive little bird with the black and chestnut tail'. In a draft of a never-published book on the birds of Cley, he continues:

> If one is patient, however, and waits quietly by the dunes or out on the flats some way from the edge of the bushes, the hungry Bluethroat will emerge into the daylight from its secret shell-paved corridors under the tangled stems and hop like a Robin on the sand, nervously flicking its tail and keeping a lustrous eye alert for any hint of danger, always ready to scuttle back into concealment on its spindly legs.

1956 saw the first of a series of large 'falls' of migrants which would characterise the late 1950s and early 1960s. 1956 saw particularly impressive numbers of Bluethroats (up to seven in a day) and Ortolan Buntings (up to three in a day) as well as Wrynecks and Barred Warblers, and a Red-breasted Flycatcher was mist-netted in the Plantation. Here indeed was an echo of the days of the gentlemen gunners, Richardson remarking enthusiastically that 2nd September of that year was a real 'old-fashioned' day.

Sadly, however, 1956 proved to be the high point of Cley Bird Observatory and its operations on Blakeney Point. On 4th November 1957 a violent gale lifted the ringing hut off its foundations, reducing it to matchwood, and also partly destroyed the trap. Richardson remained positive, however, noting in the 1957 *Norfolk Bird Report* that 'it is hoped that the Observatory will be able to continue to play an important part in the work of the fifteen ringing stations round the coast of Britain'.

The late 1950s were a fertile time for the new bird observatory movement and its fortunes went rapidly from strength to strength. As noted by Richardson, by 1957 at least fifteen observatories were in operation and in 1958 the BTO appointed ex-Fair Isle Director Kenneth Williamson as its new Migration Research Officer. In 1959 it launched a new journal *Bird Migration*, with Williamson as its first Editor. Standardised recording techniques such as daily logs and weather records were introduced and, for the first time, detailed analysis was undertaken of the movements of some of the species familiar as migrants at Blakeney Point, notably the Pied and Spotted Flycatcher, Redstart and Black Redstart and Whinchat and Ring Ousel.

Migration is, of course, complex and multi-faceted but the key focus for this generation of migration workers was the collection of data from the observatories network and the correlation of these results with the weather.

A basic understanding of the influence of weather had already been worked out by the gentlemen gunners and the early migrant-watchers. Now, however, the importance of the weather was fully confirmed. 'All our observations pointed to the strong probability that the major factor concerned was the wind', noted Williamson. More comprehensive observations and more accurate weather charts now enabled much more detailed analyses to be made and new concepts were quickly developed. Chief amongst these new ideas, and the one most directly relevant to Blakeney Point (and indeed to all the east coast observatories), was the phenomenon of 'drift migration', the process by which autumn night migrants are displaced westwards across the North Sea to Britain. This notion's chief developer and advocate was Kenneth Williamson.

A bird migrating at night, argued Williamson, flies in a 'preferred direction', correcting its course in relation to features in the landscape below. But over the largely featureless sea, and particularly in conditions of poor visibility, it will be drifted off this preferred course by the wind. The weather conditions which cause winds likely to drift birds across the North Sea are of two kinds, one 'anticyclonic', the other 'cyclonic'.

In the first of these two scenarios an anticyclone centred to the northeast of Britain (typically over Scandinavia and western Russia) will, through its cold conditions, clear skies and light northerly winds, trigger a departure of migrants to the south. On entering the easterly winds on the southern side of the anticyclone, birds will be drifted westwards and will eventually make landfall in Britain. This mechanism also brings Siberian birds (such as Yellow-browed Warblers) on what Williamson termed 'post-juvenile dispersal' rather than true migration.

The second mechanism involves a depression in the southern North Sea (typically over the Netherlands) which will displace migrant birds in the easterly winds around its northern flank. In this scenario the associated frontal cloud and rain, as it moves along the coast, may ground larger numbers of birds but it may produce fewer Siberian rarities. Of course these two synoptic situations may occur simultaneously, each reinforcing the effect of the other.

Williamson further proposed that arrivals of birds under these conditions were not entirely 'accidental' and that 'down-wind directed drift' could be regarded as a 'deliberate' migration strategy. In support of this notion he developed the concept of 'cyclonic approach', the mechanism whereby birds from

Greenland and Iceland, such as Pink-footed Geese, Wheatears and Redwings, could assist their autumn migration to Britain by using the northwesterly winds to the rear of North Atlantic depressions.

As well as documenting the movements of common migrants, the observatory workers also found a host of scarce and rare species, fully confirming the earlier discoveries of the gentlemen gunners and the first migrant-watchers. Species such as Yellow-browed Warbler and Richard's Pipit were, it turned out, of regular occurrence on our shores and even rarer birds were found too including, in 1951 at Monk's House bird observatory in Northumberland, the first British Pallas's Warbler since Ted Ramm's 1896 bird at Blakeney Point. This time, however, the bird was not shot on sight but was captured, examined and released unharmed.

The young bird observatory movement had now come of age, capturing the imagination of a whole generation of ornithologists and amateur birdwatchers. Something of the excitement of this era is captured in a series of inspiring bird observatory books, notably Eric Ennion's 1959 *The House on the Shore*, the story of Monk's House, Joe Eggeling's 1960 *The Isle of May* and Kenneth Williamson's *Fair Isle and its Birds*, published in 1965.

Key to this success was the blending of professional science with amateur enthusiasm and effort. Observatories provided the opportunity for amateurs to contribute to their work, recording and counting birds and helping with ringing activities. In return, the observatories offered training in identification and bird-handling techniques and, important in these less affluent times, they also offered a cheap holiday. The greatest attraction, however, was the birds themselves. The observatories provided the chance to see large numbers of birds, often at close quarters, and, with luck, the odd rarity or two.

Fortunately, Richardson's enthusiasm ensured that Cley Bird Observatory was still able to make a contribution. Its activities on Blakeney Point continued and autumn 1958 saw a further run of Bluethroats, with up to six in a day, as well as a Rustic

Bunting mist-netted in the Plantation. Observations from the Point now featured prominently in *Bird Migration* and in 1959 Richardson collaborated with the first radar studies of migration, carried out by David Lack of Oxford's Edward Grey Institute of Field Ornithology (and previously a pupil at Gresham's School in Holt).

In May 1960 another Subalpine Warbler was netted, and September saw up to eight Bluethroats in a day, but in 1961, on 3rd October, a much more exciting discovery was made by Barry Spence, an annual visitor to the Point and later Warden of Spurn Bird Observatory. On this day he discovered a 'strange, large, dark olive leaf warbler' at the Hood. Once mist-netted and examined in the hand it was identified as a Radde's Warbler from Siberia, only the second British record and the first in the twentieth century (the first being at North Coates, home of John Cordeaux, in October 1898). So great was the excitement over this capture that the bird was taken to Richardson's outdoor aviary in Cley and kept overnight for Williamson to see it next day.

Not everyone saw such excitements as representing progress, however. For some, the spirit and attitudes of the gentlemen gunners were not quite dead. Only days before the discovery of the Radde's Warbler, Clifford Borrer, last of the collectors, wrote disparagingly in *The Shooting Times and Country Magazine* of the 'rule of thumb quasi-scientific methods of the modern bird observatory with its heligoland traps and mist nets and ringing'. Borrer was marooned in the past, however, and Cley Bird Observatory stuck to its task. A year later, on 21st September 1962, the Hood produced the first Norfolk Yellow-browed Warbler for over forty years though it remained uncaptured, having twice flown through a mist net.

Sadly, despite these successes, Cley Bird Observatory closed in 1963. Richardson wished to retire and the then management committee could see no way to finance a replacement permanent Warden. Richardson still undertook some ringing on the Point, however, and he was present on 3rd September 1965, the day of the greatest ever 'fall' of birds which witnessed many hundreds of common migrants and at least a dozen Bluethroats.

The story of Blakeney Point as a ringing site was not quite over, however. Michael Cant took up where the observatory had left off, ringing over three thousand birds between 1966 and 1969 but by the 1970s all observatory-style observation and ringing had finally ceased.

As if to mark the end of this era, Blakeney Point's famous Bluethroats went into a steady but largely unexplained decline. The fall of 1965 was to be their final 'swansong', their last sizeable autumn arrival, and thereafter they slowly faded away. By the time of Richardson's death in 1977, the Bluethroat had become a scarce visitor.

Richardson's work on Blakeney Point had, however, made a great impact. It had breathed much-needed life into Norfolk ornithology, rescuing it from the doldrums of the 1930s and 1940s. It had repeated and confirmed the discoveries of the gentlemen gunners. It had also contributed much to our understanding of bird migration, the influence of weather and the occurrence of scarce and rare birds. Birds ringed on Blakeney Point had helped to sketch out the migration routes and destinations of many of our migrants. From its dreary Suaeda bushes, birds had gone on to sunnier climes: Redstarts to Portugal and Spain, a Redwing to France and Song Thrushes to both France and Spain. More importantly, perhaps, Richardson had inspired a whole new generation of birdwatchers who had come to know and love Blakeney Point and its migrant birds.

The eventual demise of Cley Bird Observatory also reflected broader troubles within the bird observatory movement. Two developments in particular had undermined their role. First, the introduction of easily portable mist nets meant that would-be ringers of migrant birds were no longer restricted to the bird observatory network. With the permission of a friendly landowner, migrant-ringing could now be done anywhere.

More problematic, however, were the early results from Lack's radar studies. These fully confirmed the notion of 'broad front' migration but the movements displayed on the radar screen showed little correlation with those noted at the bird observatories. Most migrants, it quickly became clear, simply overflew the coast. In comparison with the picture revealed by radar, the movements noted at the bird observatories were deemed to be both 'unrepresentative' in nature and 'trivial' in scale.

Moreover, the radar workers found no evidence of 'deliberate' down-wind directed drift as a mechanism for extending migratory flight, the notion developed by Williamson and largely accepted by observatory workers. Down-wind displacement did occur but, claimed the radar workers, it was 'accidental' and due simply to disorientation in adverse weather conditions.

These initial findings caused a rift between two of the leading protagonists of migration studies and provoked a crisis of confidence in the bird observatory movement. With hindsight, there was ample scope for collaboration. Radar workers couldn't actually identify the birds they saw flickering on their screens whilst the observatories, although they could identify the birds they were seeing, could not see the movements taking place overhead. The opportunity for productive collaboration was, however, lost.

Soon, other factors came into play as well. In the world of professional ornithology, the study of weather and migration became increasingly marginalised by rival preoccupations, by studies of breeding biology and behaviour, population and distribution. Soon, the radar work ceased, the BTO's Migration Research Officer post was discontinued and the journal *Bird Migration* was subsumed within *Bird Study*. Lack died in 1973 and Williamson in 1977.

Meanwhile birdwatching was becoming ever more popular but ever more disparate. From the 1970s onwards it took on many different, though not mutually exclusive, guises. For some it was a scientific enterprise, an exercise in data gathering for organised surveys. For others, 'twitching', the single-minded pursuit of rare birds, was the driving force. For others still, 'local patch' watching offered the greatest attraction. For many of this new generation, however, the study of migration and the weather was no longer the main focus of their interest. With more observers now active around our coasts, observatories also lost their position as the sole providers of rare birds whilst the advent of better communications and greater mobility meant that those interested in seeing them could, instead of staying and contributing to the observatory's work, just visit for an hour or two before dashing off somewhere else.

In short, migration studies and the work of bird observatories became unfashionable, out of step with contemporary concerns and interests and increasingly bypassed by both the professional ornithologist and the amateur birdwatcher. Those observatories which survived had to reinvent themselves and carve out a new role, contributing more explicitly to conservation monitoring and broadening their appeal to other constituencies.

Blakeney Point and the wider network of observatories had, however, fostered a whole generation of birdwatchers for whom the experience would remain the defining influence over their interest. They had been much more than vehicles for scientific research. Tapping into man's age-old fascination with the migrations of birds, they had been avian theatres, providing excitement, inspiration and a front row seat for some exceptional drama.

7

SEAL SANDS

We need another and a wiser and perhaps a more mystical concept of animals...

Henry Beston

Today, in a new century, Blakeney Point is still somewhere to think about our place in nature. This shingle ridge has always been synonymous with seals, and its seal-watching trips are famous, but our relationship with these animals has a long, complex and contradictory history. Here we have not only watched them for pleasure but we have also regarded them as objects of dispassionate scientific enquiry and persecuted them as hated foes, competitors for 'our' fish. The founding of a new Grey Seal colony here in 2001 is welcome but it reminds us of the many unanswered questions about our relationship with these, and indeed all, wild creatures.

Plate 13. Grey Seals on the outer beach (*Andy Stoddart*)

Plate 14. A Common Seal cull

On a cold November day the Point presents a bleak prospect: a long, wild shore stretching to the Blakeney Channel and then onward to the distant dark line of Holkham Meals. This is not a lifeless place, however. Rounding the northern end of the Sandhills one is confronted with an extraordinary sight. The whole beach, both above and below the tide line, is dotted with hundreds of great dark hulks: Grey Seals.

Since 2001, when the very first Grey Seal pup was born here, this has become a large and growing colony. From late October until January each year this is the seals' domain. Now the screaming terns and the human summer vistors have gone and the beach is theirs, shared only with the Herring Gulls at the tide edge and wandering bands of Snow Buntings along the driftline; tattered windblown fragments of life amongst the grey leviathans. For these short months Blakeney Point hosts the most important part of the seals' annual cycle. This is the time for pupping, and the scene is dominated by tiny yellowish-white pups and attentive cows, but it is also mating time and there is tension in the air as the bulls manoeuvre and fight.

The imprint of their presence is obvious on the landscape, a maze of criss-crossing sinuous tracks where the great bulls have dragged themselves into the dune grasses and the Suaeda fringe, flattening everything before them. In winter, the seals are as much a sculpting force here as the wind and tide.

The colony is a kaleidoscope of different hues. The new pups change colour rapidly from yellowish to dazzling white and then, as the moult rapidly progresses, to a pale stone-grey. The adults are almost infinitely variable, some almost black, dark as peat or rusted iron, others a pale coffee-brown, dark slate-grey, dun, tan or cream and variably patterned with mottles, rings and whirls. No two animals are alike and in their smooth forms and endless variety of colours and markings they echo the shapes and patterns of the shingle.

Up close, the seals look back at the human intruder with large, brown, liquid eyes and ever-twitching sand-caked whiskers. Glistening tears run down their cheeks whilst many of the males have necks running in blood. Downwind the air is rich with the odour of fish, faeces and afterbirth. Just as compelling is the sound of this beach, a wailing and moaning, rising and falling, so strangely human that one turns round with a start. After dark, these sounds haunt the imagination.

Thanks to science, we have learned much about seals and their evolutionary history. Some fifty million years ago some mammals returned to the sea where, eventually, they would become the seals we know today. Their skeletal structure is evidence of their terrestrial inheritance but today's seals are true creatures of the sea. Their bodies are fusiform and enclosed within a substantial layer of blubber, insulating them against the cold and streamlining their shape. This blubber helps to sustain the females during the pupping season and also the males during the mating priod. Seals' limbs are webbed between the fingers and toes and hence act as flippers. Carriage on land is therefore generally slow and awkward (though surprisingly rapid if alarmed) but in the water the seal is transformed, its rear flippers providing powerful thrust whilst its fore-flippers are used for steering.

Evolution has equipped seals well for their life in water. They can dive to depths of at least a hundred metres and remain submerged for up to twenty minutes at a time. Their blood contains very high levels of haemoglobin and they can shut off their blood supply to the muscles and internal organs when diving. This directs oxygen supply to the brain so that their heart beats at only one-tenth of the rate it does when the seal is at the surface.

Seals have an annual breeding cycle, achieved by a delay in the development of the foetus. The egg is fertilised during mating but then remains unattached in the uterus for around three months before implantation.

The seals form a discrete order of mammals - the Pinnipedia - within which our two breeding species have been allocated generic and specific names: *Halichoerus grypus,* the Grey Seal, and *Phoca vitulina,* the Common Seal. The Grey Seal is Britain's largest breeding mammal, males weighing as much as 300 kg, females betwen 150 and 200 kg. It has a long straight muzzle, giving a rather dog-like appearance, and its widely-spaced nostrils lie in parallel. The much larger males have a particularly long and convex muzzle which gives the impression of a 'Roman nose'. Grey Seals are found in three main populations, occurring on both sides of the North Atlantic and in the Baltic Sea, breeding on both rocky and sandy coasts and even on ice. As elsewhere, the British population has shown a steady increase in recent decades and three new colonies have recently been founded in the southern North Sea: at Donna Nook in Lincolnshire, at Horsey in east Norfolk and here at Blakeney Point.

The Common Seal is smaller, the male weighing up to 150 kg at most, the female up to around 100 kg. It has a small head and a concave muzzle, imparting a softer, more cat-like facial expression, and its closely-spaced nostrils form a 'V' shape. It is found in both the North Atlantic and the North Pacific where it favours sheltered, shallow waters and pups on sandy shores or even in the water. Common Seals are particularly vulnerable to pollution and disease, however, and the size of all its populations, including that in Britain, fluctuates markedly. In 1998 and 2002 outbreaks of phocine distemper virus killed many thousands of Common Seals in the North Sea.

The early status of the Grey Seal at Blakeney Point is not well documented but, until recently, it appears to have been quite rare, the Watcher Ted Eales noting only a few wanderers from the short-lived colony on Scroby Sands off Great Yarmouth. In the 1970s it was a regular but still rare visitor at Blakeney Point and even in the 1980s and 1990s it remained scarce, both here and elsewhere around the north coast. Then, in early winter 2001, the first pups were born on Blakeney Point, the foundation of the present colony. At the Point today Grey Seals are present in small numbers all year but start to come ashore at the very end of October, first the large bulls and then the females, and very soon the first pups are born. In 2012 over a thousand young seals were born here.

Despite the winter dominance of the Grey Seal today, however, the traditional seal of Blakeney Point has always been the Common Seal. These loaf around the far spits and the outer sandbanks throughout the year but only a few pup here. Most young are born in the summer on the remote sandbanks of the Wash.

There is, however, much more to the story of our seals than a collection of facts, statistics and dates. We may like to think of today's seals purely through the eyes of science but our relationship with these animals has been, in reality, a much more complex, contradictory and troubled one. We have also regarded seals with distrust and hatred, seeing them in terms of their perceived impact on fish stocks and alleged damage to economic interests. For many, the seal has been not a creature to observe and record but a hated predator, a competitor for 'our' fish.

In *Sea Swallows* Bob Pinchen refers to the presence of small numbers of Common Seals, up to fifty at a time, but even in these low numbers he notes that 'their presence was not required'. Employed as Watcher to protect the breeding terns, his sympathies did not extend to the seals, nor, of course, did those of local fishermen. The seals were widely blamed, as the terns had been, for the decline in flatfish, and for years they were clubbed and shot in the name of preserving fish stocks. Ted Eales notes in *Countryman's Memoirs* that 'they have increased so much that I think there is rather a serious problem with controlling them'. He continues: 'in the early days you could get ten shillings a nose for a seal', a reference to the Ministry of Agriculture and Fisheries bounty scheme which rewarded anyone for killing a seal and cutting its snout off. At such times, he notes, the Point's shoreline could be littered with washed-up seal carcasses.

Elsewhere too, seal-hunting remained a widespread and routine practice. A 1948 British Pathé newsreel is revealing about contemporary attitudes. It records a seal-hunting expedition by local fishermen to Scroby Sands, describing the event as a 'war on poachers of the sea'. The film claims that seals have 'so depleted fish shoals that the very livelihood of local fishermen is in peril', before concluding that 'hunting seals is not a sport for these Norfolk fishermen: their homes and families are in danger'.

Though birds had long attracted the nation's sympathy and an ever-increasing raft of protection legislation, few voices were raised in protest at the slaughter of seals. Those few who did speak out on their behalf did so not for the Common Seal but for the Grey. By the time of the First War there was concern (albeit misplaced) that the British population of this animal might be as low as five hundred animals and that it might be heading for extinction in our waters. Amongst those lobbying for protection was Charles Lyell MP who wrote to the Secretary of State for Scotland in 1913 to the effect that although they did undoubtedly take fish they were nevertheless 'quite harmless and interesting beasts'.

Although Grey Seal numbers were not, in fact, as low as had been claimed, 1914 saw the passage of the Grey Seal (Protection) Act, establishing a close season from 1st October to 15th December. This was the first protection legislation to be passed for any mammal though, of course, shooting remained entirely legal for most of the year. Initially intended to last for five years, the Act was extended and was replaced in 1932 by further legislation which lengthened the close season from 1st September to 31st December.

The pursuit of Common Seals, however, continued without restriction. 1966 saw a mushrooming of commercial seal-hunting, especially in the Wash, and the shooting of Common Seals continued on a significant scale through the late 1960s, eight hundred pups being shot in the Wash alone in 1969. For a time, the shore here was littered with bullet-ridden corpses.

Common Seals languished without any protection at all until the passage of the Conservation of Seals Act 1970 which introduced for the first time a close season for the smaller species from 1st June to 31st August. However, it left open a major concession, allowing seals to be killed even in the close season if there was evidence of direct damage to fishing interests. Licences were freely granted and the massacre continued. Common Seals were still being shot at Blakeney Point in the early 1970s while in the Wash over three hundred pups were taken in 1971 and 1972, mainly by high-powered rifle from motorised dinghies.

Meanwhile, by the 1970s Grey Seal numbers had risen to such an extent that culls were authorised on the Farne Islands at the behest of the National Trust, concerned about over-crowding and habitat degradation. Culling was also authorised in the Hebrides. Then, in 1978, the Government acceded to fishing industry requests to cull Grey Seals in Orkney, and a Norwegian firm was contracted to shoot both adults and pups on land. However, following television coverage of the cull there was a public outcry and the programme was summarily abandoned.

Norfolk's Grey Seals were also persecuted. The Scroby Sands colony had always had a troubled history. Grey Seals require solid ground on which to pup, yet Scroby was often inundated at high tide, leading to the death of new-born pups. Attempts by the seals to pup on the firmer beaches of east Norfolk were, however, usually met with a hail of bullets, a practice still prevalent as recently as the mid-1990s.

Our relationship with seals has therefore been defined as much by economics as it has by science. Even the protection legislation was driven more by economic arguments than by ethical or aesthetic considerations. It was, at heart, a utilitarian project, a programme of regulation and population control, an exercise in resource management.

However, as well as the seal of the scientist and that of the fisherman, there is another seal, the one which adorns postcards, calendars and tea towels all along this coast. This seal is a cute and unthreatening presence, an inhabitant of holiday memories and photographs. Every day in the summer, and often in the winter too, small boats leave the quaysides of Blakeney and Morston and head for the far spit and the outer sandbanks, for the seals are the definitive Blakeney Point tourist attraction, as much a feature of north Norfolk holidays as buckets and spades and ice creams. For decades excited children (and their parents) have been rewarded with intimate views of these animals against a backdrop of sunny skies, yellow sands and shrieking terns. Accustomed to their presence, the seals take little notice, merely raising an inquisitive head to stare back at the human visitors.

It is little wonder that seals are so popular with the public. Their round faces and large liquid eyes are wonderfully endearing whilst their rotund shape, awkward carriage on land and short paw-like flippers add further to the sense that these are cute pets rather than wild animals. And if the adults are endearing, how much more so are the young pups?

There is here, of course, yet another seal, the one which has provided a source of income for local families for over fifty years. With the decline in fishing, the local fishermen were quick to realise that as much money, if not more, could be made from seal-watching trips and seals are today a valuable asset, a welcome boost to the local economy.

Perhaps like nowhere else, Blakeney Point lays bare our often complicated and overlapping relationships with seals. For the biologist this is an animal to be observed, studied, counted and monitored, a finite, limited, knowable creature, capable of being defined and understood. We call this science. For the fisherman and the fisheries legislator it is a traditional foe, a hated predator, something to be persecuted, managed and controlled. We call this economic necessity. For the holidaymaker the seal is an amusing sight, a pleasant and undemanding diversion akin to a trip to the zoo. We call this recreation. For the seal trip operator it is an economic resource, a free natural asset to be jealously guarded. We call this business.

There are therefore many seals but which, if any, is the real one? We have created a variety of mental niches into which we place them but we fail consistently to see the whole animal. We see only the seal of our imagination.

In reality, of course, seals go about their business oblivious to our partial narratives, more complicated and more mysterious than we might like to admit. Can we, though, imagine the seal in other ways? Can we have a more nuanced and open-minded understanding of these animals, one which respects their existence as other beings with their own place in nature? These are questions which go back to our earliest notions not just of seals but of all animals, of what they are and of what our relationship with them should be.

Our early ideas about animals were driven by the religious doctrine of human uniqueness, the special position of superiority granted to man by God. Amongst the Church's earliest preoccupations was the desire to emphasise the gulf which existed between man and animals and to identify those attributes which most amply confirmed its existence. All sorts of human characteristics were invoked to prove this fundamental separation. Animals were guided, it was claimed, only by instinct and appetite but man was physically, intellectually and morally superior, possessing the powers of speech, reason, memory, imagination, curiosity and conscience. Above all, however, man possessed a soul, the unique distinction between himself and brute creation. Animals were, in effect, objects, there to be used according to man's whim, for food or clothing or as beasts of burden. Their only other legitimate role was that of religious symbol, to illustrate a theological point or to assist our contemplation of scripture.

The idea of animals as 'lower' creatures, as mere objects, was given further elaboration by the earliest thinkers of the

Enlightenment, the new age of science. The seventeenth century scientist and philosopher René Descartes argued that animal consciousness could be explained mechanically. Animals were, he proposed, machines or automata, like clocks, with no independent mind, let alone a soul, capable of complex behaviour but not of reasoning, perception or reflection. They were also incapable of sensation, leading to the widespread belief that they felt no pain, their cries purely unconscious reflexes.

Ever since the Enlightenment the interpretation of the natural world has been claimed by science, its approach stubbornly objective and analytical. Science encourages the belief that there is an ultimate reality which can be discerned with ever more surveillance and monitoring, ever more data and numbers. In denying the value of subjectivity, imagination, aesthetic appreciation and ethical or emotional engagement, it fuels a perspective on animals which remains detached, utilitarian and economic.

Though both religious and scientific traditions have sought to emphasise the distance between humans and animals, there have always been challenges and counter-narratives to such beliefs. Even in the seventeenth century, not all agreed with Descartes that animals could be dismissed so lightly, and some began to wonder too whether the Church's gulf between men and animals might also be too rigid and too wide. Perhaps the boundary was more indistinct than the theologians and the scientists would have us believe. Perhaps the differences were only a matter of degree rather than of kind. Perhaps animals might, after all, be able to think and feel pain. As well as being threats and competitors, might animals also share much of the human experience of the world? Might they have not just a utilitarian function but also a spiritual dimension and a cultural value? Might they, rather than inferior beings, be fellow travellers worthy of respect?

Amongst the earliest to explore some other aspects of our relationship with animals was the French Renaissance essayist Michel de Montaigne. In his considerations of human nature and the place of animals he rejects the anthropocentric orthodoxy, asking:

> How does he know, by the strength of his understanding, the secret and internal motions of animals, and from what comparisons between them and us does he conclude the stupidity he attributes to them?

Many such ideas are, of course, implicit in traditional fable and legend. Even more than the Hare, the seal has always been a magical creature, particularly prominent in the mythology of the Celtic fringe. Here, its voices have been represented as those of drowned sailors whilst it has taken on other roles too, as mermaid or fabled 'selkie'. Recurring threads in seal legends are their ability to leave the sea and become, at least for a time, part of the human world.

By far the most remarkable and most authentic account of such legends is contained in David Thomson's 1954 *The People of the Sea*, an exploration of the place of seals in the fast-disappearing oral tradition of Shetland, Orkney, the Hebrides and the west of Ireland. In journeys around this Atlantic margin he documents his conversations with local people and conjures up a beguiling blend of history and folklore, fact and fiction, reality and fantasy. This is a world where sailors are rescued by seals, infants are suckled by seal-mothers and men take seals for wives. In his Introduction Thomson writes:

> As to the seals themselves, no scientific study can dissolve their mystery. Land animals may play their role in legend, but none, not even the hare, has such a dream-like effect on the human mind; and so, though many creatures share with them a place in our unconscious mind, a part in ancient narrative, the seal legend is unique.

It is, however, the nature writers who have been most active in exploring our complex relationship with animals. In *The Outermost House*, published in 1928, Henry Beston writes that:

We patronize them for their incompleteness, for their tragic fate of having taken form so far below ourselves. And therein we err, and greatly err. For the animal shall not be measured by man. In a world older and more complete than ours they move finished and complete, gifted with extensions of the senses we have lost or never attained, living by voices we shall never hear. They are not brethren, they are not underlings; they are other nations, caught with ourselves in the net of life and time, fellow prisoners of the splendour and travail of the earth.

Such themes are constant in the work of Barry Lopez. In his 1978 book *Of Wolves and Men* he writes of our complex relationship with the Wolf and the different roles it has played in human culture, as an object of scientific study, as a feared and despised predator and as a creature of symbol and myth. There are many clear parallels here with our relationships with seals.

Lopez's essays also address these ideas. In *The Lives of Seals* he confronts the moral and ethical issues arising from the 'collecting' of seals for conservation research in the Arctic whilst *A Presentation of Whales* recounts a beaching of Sperm Whales and our struggles to rationalise and respond to the event, whether as scientist, Government official, journalist or onlooker.

In his 1986 *Arctic Dreams*, winner of the American National Book Award, Lopez contrasts the scientific approach to animals with that of native peoples. In its focus on species and populations, and on concepts such as breeding ecology and predator-prey relationships, science regards animals as interchangeable objects from which wider understandings can be extrapolated. It frowns on the notion that they might behave as individuals, dismissing such ideas as dangerous and 'unscientific' anthropomorphism.

However, argues Lopez, the scientist's data and statistics may mask a deeper reality. Native people report that individual animals may behave differently at different times and and in different places and that they can display motive and intention. Should we, perhaps, be more prepared to speak of individual animals rather than of a collective entity? Is it possible that animals are not uniform, identical beings but that they are instead, as we are, individuals, living, breathing, constantly responding to our environment?

Along the Point's outer beach, no more than a few yards offshore, a Grey Seal raises its head out of the water. It is difficult to look away for its stare carries meaning, curiosity certainly but perhaps other intentions too. This is not an accidental encounter. The seal has noted a human presence and come in to shallow water to intercept its progress. Confronted with those great dark, liquid eyes, the urge to communicate is momentarily compelling. Is there any communication, any mutual understanding here? Is there a meeting of minds as well as eyes? Or are such thoughts merely anthropomorphic fantasy?

At home in its natural element, the seal shows no fear. It looks away, submerges and then surfaces once more. What does it think? What does it expect from this encounter? Is it surprised, troubled, disappointed? Staring into its eyes it is hard not to wonder, to search for meaning, even for dialogue. In such moments, seals remind us of our close relationship as intelligent mammals and of our own aquatic ancestry. We are also invited to consider another idea, that of a relationship which no longer projects onto these animals our prejudices and our fears but one which restores to them respect and returns them to a place of mystery.

8

MINDSCAPE

Landscapes are culture before they are nature.

Simon Schama

As well as animals, Blakeney Point also asks us about our long and complex relationship with landscape. Regarded until as recently as the mid-twentieth century as remote, marginal and unappealing, conforming to neither of the historical notions of the 'picturesque' or the 'sublime', this shingle ridge has today been transformed into an attractive 'designer destination'. A hundred years after its acquisition for essentially scientific reasons, we now view the Point through very different eyes. We are reminded here that it is ultimately culture which frames landscapes. We value places not according to how they really are but according to how they are perceived.

Plate 15. The Watch House (*Andy Stoddart*)

Plate 16. View across the Harbour (*Andy Stoddart*)

A 2012 press article to celebrate the hundredth anniversary of the National Trust's acquisition of Blakeney Point describes it as 'a polished medal on the lapel of Nelson's county' and a 'spectacular sand and shingle spit... blessed with enviable beauty'. It continues:

> On its northern side, the moody sea laps or lashes at the shingle. And the view from the south of the Point is arguably unrivalled - a magical merger of marshes, coastal creeks, varied vessels and the distant dwellings of Morston and Blakeney, nestling in the cup of the land's hand.

Such comments are not unwarranted. In high summer Blakeney Point is a riot of colour. Seaward lies blue water, gently lapping surf and a long, golden strand. Along the ridge the eye falls on a profusion of flowers: Yellow Horned-poppy, Sea Aster and Common Ragwort. To the south lies a haze of purple Sea-lavender and the shining mirror of Blakeney Harbour, dotted with white boat sails. Beyond lies the soft, gently rolling landscape of north Norfolk, the distinctive white sails of Cley mill, the tall, square tower of Blakeney church and the clusters of red pantiles which mark the coastal settlements.

Such descriptions of Blakeney Point, and indeed of all our wild places, are now routine, the accepted way in which our culture frames such places. Blakeney Point is today the 'jewel in the crown' of what has become rebranded as the 'Saltmarsh Coast'. In only thirty years this coast, with its cluster of once-working villages and thriving ports, has become the retreat of second-home-owners and summer tourists. Since the 1970s the Point has become a haven for birdwatchers, sailors, seal-watchers and walkers, and the wider coast has become a popular holiday destination and a desirable retirement retreat. North Norfolk has been reinvented as a playground for the comfortably-off, a 'colour supplement' confection of wild, romantic beaches and sand dunes, picturesque beach huts and charming flint-clad architecture, a 'designer destination' offering a flirtation with the wild but with all the comforts of home: cosy accommodation, 'high-end' dining and shopping for paintings and pots.

The coast has also been blessed by officialdom, receiving a string of designations for the perceived high quality of its landscapes. It is now an 'Area of Outstanding Natural Beauty' and a 'Heritage Coast'. Its marshland coast is 'the finest of its kind in these islands and probably in Europe', says Natural England, 'a last true wilderness in lowland Britain'. Today such responses are taken for granted. Indeed it seems remarkable that we have ever imagined this stretch of coast as anything other than a place of penetrating beauty. Such appreciation, however, has very shallow roots indeed.

For our earliest ancestors the natural world was a very different place. Wilderness as we currently understand it was a wholly meaningless concept. There was no dividing line between man and nature. Nature was simply where we lived and we were part of it. Soon, however, a physical distinction between managed and wild land began to grow. Clearing the land for settlement, domestic animals and agriculture started to create a distance, a difference, between man and nature, between what was ours and what was nature's, between what was 'tame' and what was 'wild'.

Clearing the land for dwellings, animals and crops represented the throwing back of the wilderness, both in reality and, perhaps even more importantly, in the mind. Wild land and animals were now not just the opposite of their managed, domesticated counterparts but were increasingly reinvented as a threat, as something to be kept at bay behind a fence or a wall. What lay beyond this divide became less known, more dangerous and more feared. Eventually the natural world would become a dismal and frightening place, a 'dark and howling wilderness', the haunt of wild beasts and demons.

This growing mental opposition to nature received considerable reinforcement from religious tradition. In the eyes of the Church too, man was separate from nature. Fundamental to its teachings was the notion of a Paradise, a pastoral idyll, a bountiful and fruitful garden, enclosed and protected from the savage wilderness beyond. But this was no earthly Paradise, indeed the Church strongly resisted any such notion as a distraction from man's true task on earth. The proper occupation of the Christian was the pursuit of personal spiritual correctness in preparation for the next life, not an aesthetic engagement with the natural world. Eden and the Promised Land were only to be gained through hard personal struggle, not through the appreciation of nature.

For much of our history the most prized environments have been man-made. Urban scenes have always been the most reassuring, symbolising both security and human achievement in holding back the wilderness. Cities have signified learning and sophistication, a world away from the poor manners and rustic boorishness of the countryside. However, the eighteenth century onwards saw a progressive reinvention of the rural landscape.

This rediscovery, though, did not extend to the whole of the countryside. Most valued were not nature's wilder reaches but the tamed, enclosed and 'improved' agricultural land. Here, the straight lines of hedges, crops and orchards marked the separation of culture from nature and demonstrated man's superiority and control. Beauty in the countryside came from fertility and productive use, not from abandonment to nature's confusion. 'I have no idea of picturesque beauty separate from fertility of soil', wrote William Cobbett. By contrast, wild nature was viewed with horror. It was rough, rugged, barren and thoroughly unpleasant. Of the Scottish Highlands, Dr. Johnson noted that 'an eye accustomed to flowery pastures and waving harvests is astonished by this wide extent of hopeless sterility'.

A similarly negative view of the coast prevailed. The ocean was regarded with hostility, an infinite, unknowable expanse, a restless, threatening presence and an instrument of punishment prone to sudden bursts of fury. The shoreline was a cold, unappealing place, a residue of the Flood and a reminder of its potential return. Here, on arid lonely beaches, sun-bleached and windswept, monotonous waves broke with a dismal sound, mysterious tides ebbed and flowed and the waters cast up excreta from the abyss. Here there was no bird song, only the harsh cry of gulls.

The key to the further reinvention of the countryside was the notion of the 'picturesque'. The term was first used in the clergyman William Gilipn's 1768 *Essay on Prints* in which he sets out his 'principles of picturesque beauty', defining it as 'a term expressive of that peculiar kind of beauty, which is agreeable in a picture'. The most attractive and highly valued scenery, argued Gilpin, contained those landscape features which lent themselves most readily to artistic composition, to the framed view.

Landscape art, the process of turning 'land' into 'landscape' has always been one of the most important ways in which we have responded to nature. Unsurprisingly, therefore, nature was deemed to be at its best when it most resembled a painting. Most prized of all were the classical Italian scenes popularised by seventeenth century artists, most notably Claude Lorrain. These images inspired not just a delight in rural scenery but a whole new fashion for landscaped gardens.

This artistic model implied a certain scenic variety and tonal contrast, an intricacy of composition and an obvious subject or focus of attention. The ideal landscape should have 'side screens' and a well-defined foreground, middleground and background. Its key components were of necessity vertical: a lofty mountain peak, a dramatic tree or, better still, a ruined castle on a promonotory. Coastal views could also be embraced by these new rules but only where there was a ready-made composition. Rocks and cliffs, ruggedness and an intricate intermingling of sea and land were minimum requirements.

The picturesque view of nature was, above all, formulaic, a celebration not of the character or scenic attributes of a particular place but of its conformity with a preconceived model of aesthetic harmony based on no particular location at all. Some places, of course, refused to conform to this artistic template. Flat, open, horizontal country presented no ready visual organisation and was therefore ignored. Here, with no framed view, the eye could drift and lose itself.

But there were also some rival interpretations of nature. The Romantic movement rejected the contemporary fashion for neoclassical formality and its reliance on artistic models. The Romantics celebrated not a 'picturesque' or 'beautiful' version of the natural world but nature in its raw, primitive state, informal, irregular and, above all, wild. Nature was now reinvented as 'sublime': elemental, awe-inspiring, dramatic, spiritual, powerful, full of mystery, chaos and danger, with the power to compel and destroy. The chief architect of this notion was Edmund Burke. In his 1757 *A Philosophical Enquiry into the Origin of Our Ideas of the Sublime and Beautiful* he sets out his ideas. The natural world, argued Burke, should inspire in the viewer a 'pleasant horror', a feeling of terror but also a pleasure from the knowledge that the danger is imaginary. The types of landscape most likely to produce such a thrill were grand, imposing crags, soaring, snow-capped peaks, tumbling waterfalls and cool, lush forests. The author and minister Hugh Blair asked:

> What are the scenes of nature that elevate the mind in the highest degree, and produce the sublime sensation? Not the gay landscape, the flowery field, or the flourishing city; but the hoary mountain, and the solitary lake; the aged forest, and the torrent falling over the rock.

For many, the coast was also capable of stirring such emotions, particularly vertiginous cliffs, wildly crashing surf and hidden coves. For some, even a flat shoreline could induce sensations of the sublime. Here could be seen at first hand the sea's terrifying immensity and the power of storms.

The ideas of the picturesque and the sublime created a whole new fashion for landscape tourism. Scenic tours became popular, mainly to the wilder reaches of Britain's north and west, to the Wye Valley, Snowdonia, the Lake District, the Scottish Highlands and the Hebrides. Further afield, a new generation of landscape admirers flocked to the scenic splendour of the Rhine Valley, the Alps and the Italian coast.

Unsurprisingly, East Anglia did not feature on many itineraries. Here, the lean, spare landscape of open fields and meagre hedges flouted all the definitions of the picturesque and offered little to invoke sensations of the sublime. Devoid of artistic potential, the region's horizontal landscapes were despised as the very antithesis of a beautiful view. Gilpin's assessment was damning, calling them 'chalky, bare, exposed, ridgy and unpleasant'. He was particularly disparaging about the Fens whilst Breckland was dismissed as 'wild, open and dreary'. Only a few places attracted the eye. In Dedham Vale, on the border of Suffolk and Essex, Gilpin praised the 'pleasing sylvan scenes' in what would become 'Constable Country' and, in northeast Norfolk, the cliffs at Cromer were sufficiently high to qualify as sublime. Of the latter, the *Monthly Register* of 1803 noted that:

> The cliff itself is bold and more rough and lofty than upon any other part of the eastern coast; as it is seen from the sands below it excites in the mind of the spectator the emotion which is usually inspired by the sublime.

The low, flat north Norfolk coast was, however, ignored and it barely features in the history of landscape painting. The nineteenth century 'Norwich School' of artists portrayed the conventionally picturesque scenes to be found amongst the heaths, woods and meandering rivers around Norwich. When they chose to depict the coast, it was the busy sea-front at Great Yarmouth and Gorleston and the cliffs of Cromer which most appealed.

To most eyes, therefore, Blakeney Point simply formed part of a wider, visually unappealing landscape. In the popular imagination it was remote, marginal and an aesthetic problem. Late nineteenth century attempts by the journalist Clement Scott to market the stretch of cliff-bound coast around Sheringham and Cromer as 'Poppyland' only served to further marginalise the adjacent coastline. The attractions of Poppyland were not its proximity to remote beaches and wild saltmarshes but its conformity with the picturesque: its varied and richly textured scenery, its dramatic cliffs, its pleasing ridge of pine trees and its fields of waving poppies. As Scott himself noted: 'No one thought of going beyond the lighthouse; that was the boundary of all investigation. Outside that mark the county, the farms and the villages were as lonely as in the Highlands'. Here dwelt 'Old Shuck', a huge and ghostly black dog with flaming eyes whose mythology was transplanted to Dartmoor by Conan Doyle and incorporated into *The Hound of the Baskervilles*.

The first recognition of north Norfolk, indeed of any flat coast, as an area of landscape quality only came in the twentieth century. The fashion for seaside holidays and beach-bathing was by now long-established but such tourism had always remained confined to the recognised resorts. Here, that meant the railway-served towns of Cromer and Hunstanton. Cley and Blakeney only became established as destinations in their own right in the 1920s, the catalyst being the opening of the Blakeney Hotel in 1923. Even then, however, the number of visitors was modest. A 1924 newspaper notes that 'in the summer... Cley is invaded by an army from Chelsea' but that 'the season of invasion is short; and for ten months of the year Cley is left to itself'. At this time, notes the article, 'the sea growls menacingly' and 'the marshes and banks are trodden only by those who carry guns or desire to carry home driftwood'.

Much of how we think about landscapes and what we value about them derives from how they have been portrayed and described. In this context, the fact that north Norfolk's flat shorelines remained studiously ignored by artists speaks volumes. In the absence of traditional visual portrayals, the clearest insights into the shifting visual appeal of this coast are provided by writers.

Amongst the best-known literary interpreters of the coast is the controversial author Henry Williamson. Already well known for *Tarka the Otter,* in 1936 he bought Old Hall Farm at Stiffkey, directly facing the tip of Blakeney Point. Here he wrote *The Story of a Norfolk Farm*, an account of his experiences in attempting to rescue a run-down farming operation. However, his depiction of his new surroundings is unremittingly negative, reinforcing the popular image of a wild and backward land. Blakeney Point's very first appearance in his book is a gloomy one, portrayed not as a land of sunlit beaches or enchanting marshes but as a historical landmark for German Zeppelins, a dark, brooding presence befitting an unloved, unfashionable landscape:

> Zeppelins used to make their landfall at dusk along the coast, waiting there until dark, when they moved inland to their raids. Often they were low, two or three thousand feet only above the Point.

Williamson notes 'vast tracts of marshes stretching to the sea'. 'They were grey', he writes, 'and somewhat dull'. He confirms the prevailing image of a cold and raw land, bleak, unwelcoming and unforgiving. It is contrasted repeatedly with his beloved Devon and its cosy, pastoral landscape where 'the strong green grass, nourished by the lusty, southern sun and warm ocean rains, fattens bullocks of itself'. His despair of his new surroundings continues: 'How different from Devon, with its small, hilly fields and great stone-banked hedges, rushing streams and soft moist air'. Even his mother has aesthetic problems with the landscape, complaining that 'the sun is in the wrong place. It sets over the land!'

Even in brief moments of apparent happiness, Williamson's thoughts are not on the aesthetic attractions of his present surroundings but on his childhood memories of a quite different landscape:

> We sat down on the grass, gazing out over the marshes, one vast gut-channered prairie of pale blue sea-lavender... This was the sun I remembered from boyhood days, the ancient harvest sunshine of that perished time when the earth was fresh and summer seemed an illimitable shining that would never end, the reapers moving round the fields and setting up the stooks of golden corn. And sitting there, it was as though the past and present were one again, and I had entered upon my heritage of happiness.

Williamson's attempts to farm his land at Stiffkey during the agricultural depression of the late 1930s were dogged by poor land, bad weather, an intransigent tenant and a collapse in the barley price, and his negative experiences are echoed in the picture he paints of north Norfolk as remote, backward and feudal, a rough and ready backwater where people eked out an existence on an inhospitable, lawless margin. This is an image of north Norfolk which dates back at least to Daniel Defoe's *A tour thro' the whole island of Great Britain*, written in the 1720s. For Williamson, this is a place truly stuck in the past, 'a land let go', an allegory of his political views of pre-war Britain. Finally, he turns his back on his doomed farming venture and returns to Devon. *The Story of a Norfolk Farm* is, in the end, a story of gloom, failure and retreat.

More recently, Blakeney Point has again played the role of forbidding wartime presence. In Jack Higgins's 1975 novel *The Eagle Has Landed*, the German spy Joanna Grey notes:

> It was a strange, alien world of sea creeks and mudflats and great pale barriers of reeds higher than a man's head, inhabited only by the birds, curlew and redshank and brent geese coming south from Siberia to winter on the mud flats... In the distance she could see the Point on the other side of the estuary, curving in like a great bent forefinger, enclosing an area of channels and sandbanks and shoals that, on a rising tide, was probably as lethal as anywhere on the Norfolk coast.

Some did manage to write a little more favourably of their encounters, however. In 1928 Edward Frederic (Fred) Benson included 'A Tale of an Empty House' in his collection *Spook Stories*. Benson was a regular visitor to Blakeney at the beginning of its new incarnation as a tourist resort and he sets his ghost story on the Point (known here as 'Riddington Point'). On his arrival in 'Riddington', Benson's narrator notes 'a limitless expanse of shining grasses with tufts of shrubby growth, and great patches of purple sea-lavender. Beyond were tawny sand-banks, and further yet a line of shingle and scrub and sand-dunes'. His description continues:

That line of shingle and scrub and sand dunes on the horizon was a peninsula running for four or five miles parallel with the land, forming the true beach, and it enclosed this vast basin of sand-banks and mud-banks and level lavender-covered marsh, which was submerged at high tide, and made an estuary. At low tide it was altogether empty but for the stream that struggled out through various channels to the mouth of it two miles away to the left.

Benson casts the Watch House as the archetypal horror story location. It had, he notes 'an indefinable look of desertion, as if man had attempted to domesticate himself here and had failed'. Referring to its solitariness as an 'abominable desolation', he conjectures that if one was 'forced to spend the night here, how the mind would long for any companionship, how sinister would become the calling of the birds, how weird the whistle of the wind round the cavern of this abandoned habitation'. Here, he concludes, lurked 'an awful spiritual presence'.

Such are the necessary conventions of a ghost story, however, (and it can reasonably be argued that the Watch House lends itself to such a treatment) and Benson's portrayal of the rest of Blakeney Point is a little more benign. It was, he notes, 'so immense and so empty; it had the allure of the desert about it, with none of the desert's intolerable monotony'. Here lay a 'beckoning immensity of lavender-covered, bird-haunted expanse'. Benson is clearly more captivated than repelled by the landscape. He speaks of 'the fall of dusk on the lonely marshes, their huge emptiness and their ineffable magic'. He continues:

> There was not a sign of any living human being within sight, but never have I found myself in so exhilarating a solitude. Right and left were spread the lawns of sea-lavender, starred with pink tufts of thrift and thickets of suaeda bushes... Curlews were bubbling, and redshank and ringed plover fluting, and now as I trudged up the shingle bank, at the bottom of which the marsh came to an end, the sea, blue and waveless, lay stretched and sleeping, bordered by a strip of sand, on which far off a mirage hovered. But from end to end of it, as far as eye could see, there was no sign of human presence.

Lilias Rider Haggard also wrote of this stretch of coast at the same time as Williamson though hers is a more appreciative representation. 'It was one of those rare winter days', she writes, 'a still day, cold with that clean coldness which seems to come straight from the polar ice, but with a brilliant sun'. She writes of Brent Geese 'stringing out in great skeins across the pale winter sky, swinging over the Point seawards'. 'Some enchantment', she concludes, 'lies upon the north Norfolk coast'.

It is, however, not until the post-war period that we can begin to discern a more widespread recognition of the attractions of Blakeney Point and of the coast beyond. In 1947 A.G.P. Powell writes:

> Here, where the sun beats down beneficially, and the health-giving sea breezes blow continuously, one may lie up with a pair of glasses secure in a sand-dune or beneath a sheltering bush and ponder on the mysteries of nature, or, content and at ease, feast one's eyes on the colour of the landscape, and the views inland across the marshes to the woods and cornfields of the mainland, interspersed with red-roofed villages, rising to the skyline beyond, and find that peace and refreshment which is beyond all price.

An appreciation of this landscape is taken to somewhat more gushing heights in the writings of Reginald Gaze, a summer Warden at the Point both before and after the Second War. His evident delight in his surroundings leaps from the pages of his *Bird Sanctuary*, also published in 1947:

> A narrow strip of shingle turning in at the finish, hook-shaped, towards the Morston-Stiffkey shore; upon this a short sand dune, crowned with marram grass; the silver sand of the dunes, the golden sands left by the receding tide upon which the seals bask, on the far side of the channel; the stir and whisper of the breeze through the grey-green marrams; the ceaseless murmur of the sea against the far sands; white wings against a deep blue sky; the harsh cries of the wheeling terns... this is the Bird Sanctuary on Blakeney Point.

He continues in similar vein:

> When does one see the Point at its best? In summer when the skies are blue and terns scream, dive, fight and play overhead and seals bask in the sunshine on the sandbanks; or when skies are grey and lowering in a bitter north-easter with strings of geese honking overhead, and the frosts have turned the tips of the suaeda bushes, reds and golds and russets.

The following year, *Redshank's Warning* was published by the children's author Malcolm Saville. Here the Point is portrayed as a remote and exciting place, a children's adventure playground. The child characters find that 'as soon as they left the foreshore and took the rough cart track which led them out on to the Point, it seemed as if they were in a different world'. Here, they note with delight:

> The occasional cry of the birds, the distant murmur of the sea, and the song of the wind in the grass were the only sounds to break the silence... Only in a place like this could you really *smell* fresh air!

A more contemporary account is given by Richard Mabey in *Home Country*. He describes birdwatching here as a boy with Richard Richardson ('a cross between Mr. Punch and a weatherbeaten rocker') but his main focus is on the landscape, a place literally 'on the edge'. Here, notes Mabey, lies 'a frayed margin, of opportunity and possibilities'. At first he struggles to adjust to his surroundings: 'I'd found the marsh landscape incomprehensible at first, too huge and incoherent to be anything other than a backdrop. But it had that twice-daily refashioning by the tide, and as I got used to its rhythms, it began to seem less foreign'. He sees:

> ... an astonishing panorama - a mile of saltmarsh shimmering under a high tide... Out in the distance, framed against the breakers, we could just make out Blakeney Point, the shingle spit that was all that separated the harbour from the German Ocean. It was a sight that has kept me in thrall to this coast ever since, a liberating vision of being at the edge of things.

Today, Blakeney Point's long, lonely beaches and the twisting labyrinth of its saltmarsh creeks, the flat horizon and the relentless sky - the very features which have traditionally led to aesthetic marginalisation - have been embraced with enthusiasm and delight. These once-despised landscape features have been reinvented as scenic and desirable, even as picturesque.

A new eco-awareness, an increased affluence and the area's accessibility to London have all played their part in this transformation. But this is not just a social and economic phenomenon. Changing aesthetic fashions have been perhaps the dominant influence. Fashions are, however, transitory, and there are threats to our current perceptions of the coast. The increase in the number of visitors may adversely impact on the very sense of landscape quality and remoteness which people come here to experience. Offshore, the appearance of windfarms has changed the visual character of the coast and has the potential to change it further.

Like all landscapes, Blakeney Point has always been, and will continue to be, shaped by the place it occupies in our imagination, by what we see, how we see it and what we choose to value. When we look at nature we select, edit, suppress and emphasise elements of what we see. Without even being aware of it, we are shaping and interpreting, bringing our cultural heritage with us.

A landscape is, we learn here, a cultural construct, a perceived condition as much as an actual one, an idea as much as reality. Landscapes are artefacts of our perception, blank canvases onto which we project our ideas. They are, in the end, whatever we think they are.

BIBLIOGRAPHY

Allison, H. & Morley, J. (eds.). 1989. *Introduction to Blakeney Point and Scolt Head Island*. National Trust, Norfolk.

Andrews, M. 1999. *Landscape and Western Art*. Oxford University Press, Oxford.

Arnold, E.C. 1947. *Memories of Cley*. Baskerville Press, Eastbourne.

Ayres, P.G. 2012. *Shaping Ecology*: *The Life of Arthur Tansley*. John Wiley & Sons, Ltd.

Barfoot, P.J. & Tucker, J.J. Geomorphological Changes at Blakeney Point, Norfolk. *Transactions of the Norfolk & Norwich Naturalists' Society* 25: 49-60.

Benson, E.F. 1928. *Spook Stories*. London Hutchinson, London.

Beston, H. 1928. *The Outermost House*: *A Year of Life on the Great Beach of Cape Cod*. Henry Holt & Co., New York.

Bird, E.C.F. & Wain, J. 1963. Changes at Blakeney Point since 1953. *Transactions of the Norfolk & Norwich Naturalists' Society* 20: 1.

Bishop, B. & Bishop, B. 1996. *Cley Marsh and Its Birds*. Hill House Press, Holt.

Bjärvall, A. & Ullström, S. 1986. *The Mammals of Britain and Europe*. Croom Helm Ltd., Beckenham.

Blanning, T. 2010. *The Romantic Revolution*. Weidenfeld & Nicolson, London.

Brooks, P. 1984. *Cley: Living with Memories of Greatness*. Poppyland Publishing, North Walsham.

Buell, L. 1995. *The Environmental Imagination: Thoreau, Nature Writing and the Formation of American Culture*. Harvard University Press, London.

Burke, E. 1757. *A Philosophical Enquiry into the Origin of Our Ideas of the Sublime and Beautiful.*

Carey, A.E. & Oliver, F.W. 1918. *Tidal Lands: A Study of Shore Problems*. Blackie, London.

Clarke, W.E. 1912. *Studies in Bird Migration*. Oliver & Boyd, Edinburgh.

Corbin, A. 1994. *The Lure of the Sea: the Discovery of the Seaside 1750-1840*. Penguin, London.

Cutright, P.R. & Brodhead, M.J. 2001. *Elliott Coues: Naturalist and Frontier Historian*. University of Illinois Press, Urbana and Chicago.

Defoe, D. 1724-27. *A Tour thro' the whole island of Great Britain*.

Dorst, J. 1956. *The Migrations of Birds*. William Heinemann Ltd., London.

Dresser, H.E. 1897. Notes on Pallas's Willow Warbler and some other rare European warblers. *Transactions of the Norfolk & Norwich Naturalists' Society* 6: 280-290.

Durman, R. (ed.). 1976. *Bird Observatories in Britain and Ireland*. T. & A.D. Poyser Ltd., Berkhamsted.

Eales, W.E.R. 1986. *Memoirs of a Countryman*: *A Warden's Life on Blakeney Point*. Jim Baldwin Publishing, Fakenham.

Elkins, N. 1983. *Weather and Bird Behaviour*. T. & A.D. Poyser Ltd., Calton.

Ennion, E.A. 1959. *The House on the Shore*. Routledge & Kegan Paul Ltd., London.

Evans, A. 1992. *A History of Nature Conservation in Britain*. Routledge, London.

Fisher, J. 1966. *The Shell Bird Book*. Ebury Press & Michael Joseph, London.

Gätke, H. 1895. *The Birds of Heligoland*. David Douglas, Edinburgh.

Gaze, J. 1988. *Figures in a Landscape*: *A History of the National Trust*. Barrie & Jenkin, London.

Gaze, R. 1947. *Bird Sanctuary*. Faber & Faber Ltd., London.

Gilpin, W. 1768. *Essay on Prints.*

Gombrich, E.H. 1950. *The Story of Art*. Phaidon Press Ltd., London.

Harrap, S. 2008. *Flowers of the Norfolk Coast*. Norfolk Nature, Holt.

Higgins, J. 1975. *The Eagle Has Landed*. Collins, London.

Hudson, W.H. 1913. *Adventures Among Birds*. Hutchinson & Co., London.

Leopold, A. 1933. *Game Management.* New York: Scribner.

Leopold, A. 1949. *A Sand County Almanac*. Oxford University Press, Oxford.

Lloyd, C. 1985. *The Travelling Naturalists*. Croom Helm, London.

Lockley, R.M. 1966. *Grey Seal, Common Seal*. Andre Deutsch, London.

Lopez, B. 1978. *Of Wolves and Men*. Charles Scribner's Sons, New York.

Lopez, B. 1986. *Arctic Dreams*: *Imagination and Desire in a Northern Landscape*. Macmillan, London.

Lopez, B. 1989. *Crossing Open Ground*. Vintage Books, New York.

Mabey, R. 1990. *Home Country*. Random Century Group, London.

Macfarlane, R. 2004. *Mountains of the Mind*: *A History of a Fascination*. Granta Books, London.

Macfarlane, R. 2008. *The Wild Places*. Granta Books, London.

May, V.J. & Hansom, J.D. 2003. *Coastal Geomorphology of Great Britain*. Geological Conservation Review Series No. 28. Joint Nature Conservation Committee, Peterborough.

McCallum, J. 2012. *The Long, Wild Shore*: *Bird and Seal Seasons on Blakeney Point*. Silver Brant, Holt.

McConnell, B. 1988. The Common Seal Disaster. *Norfolk Bird & Mammal Report* 1988. Norfolk & Norwich Naturalists's Society.

Mearns, B. & Mearns, R. 1998. *The Bird Collectors*. Academic Press, London.

Meeres, F. 2010. *The North Norfolk Coast*. Phillimore & Co., Andover.

Moore, N.W. 1987. *The Bird of Time*: *the science and politics of nature conservation*. Cambridge University Press, Cambridge.

Moss, S. 2004. *A Social History of Birdwatching*. Aurum Press Ltd., London.

Nash, R.F. 2001. *Wilderness and the American Mind*. Yale University Press, Yale.

Oliver, F.W. 1912. The shingle beach as a plant habitat. *New Phytologist* 11: 73-99.

Oliver, F.W. & Salisbury, E.J. 1913. The topography and vegetation of the National Trust reserve, known as Blakeney Point. *Transactions of the Norfolk & Norwich Naturalists' Society* 9: 485-542.

Oliver, F.W. 1913. Some Remarks on Blakeney Point, Norfolk. *Journal of Ecology* 1: 4-15.

Oliver, F.W. & Salisbury, E.J. Vegetation and mobile ground as illustrated by *Suaeda fruticosa* on shingle. *Journal of Ecology* 1: 249-272.

Oliver, F.W. (ed.). 1917. *The Exploitation of Plants*. J.M. Dent & Sons Ltd., London.

Pashley, H.N. 1925. *Notes on the Birds of Cley*. Witherby, London.

Pearson, J., Taylor, K., Woodall, J. & Hovill, D. 2007. An annotated list of the plants of Blakeney Point, Norfolk, with selected distribution maps. *Transactions of the Norfolk & Norwich Naturalists' Society* 40: 16-54.

Pinchen, R.J. 1935. *Sea Swallows*. Green & Co. Ltd.

Power, F.D. 1885. Ornithological Notes at Cley and Blakeney September 3rd to 19th 1884. *Transactions of the Norfolk & Norwich Naturalists' Society* 4: 36-43.

Richardson, R.A. 1962. *Checklist of the Birds of Cley and Neighbouring Parishes*. Cley Bird Observatory.

Rowan, W. 1918. An Annotated List of the Birds of Blakeney Point, Norfolk. *Transactions of the Norfolk & Norwich Naturalists' Society* 10: 256-279.

Salisbury, E.J. 1952. Francis Wall Oliver 1864-1951. *Obituary Notices of Fellows of the Royal Society* 8: 229-240.

Saville, M. 1948. *Redshank's Warning*. Lutterworth Press, London.

Schama, S. 1995. *Landscape and Memory*. HarperCollins *Publishers*, London.

Scott, I. & Worsley, R. 2010. *The Return of the Tide*. JJG Publishing, Hindringham.

Seebohm, H. 1985. *The Birds of Siberia: To the Petchora Valley*. Alan Sutton Publishing Ltd., Gloucester.

Sheail, J. 1976. *Nature in Trust*. Blackie & Son Ltd., Glasgow.

Steers, J.A. (ed.). 1934. *Scolt Head Island*. Heffer & Sons Ltd., Cambridge.

Steers, J.A. (ed.). 1946. *The Coastline of England and Wales*. Cambridge University Press, Cambridge.

Steers, J.A. 1953. *The Sea Coast*. Collins, London.

Stoddart, A.M. & Joyner, S.C. 2005. *The Birds of Blakeney Point*. Wren Publishing, Sheringham.

Stubbings, E. 2012. The Birds of Blakeney Point: 100 years of National Trust ownership. *British Birds* 105: 497-554.

Tansley, A.G. 1904. The Problems of Ecology. *New Phytologist* 3: 191-200.

Tansley, A.G. 1935. The Use and Abuse of Vegetational Concepts and Terms. *Ecology* 16: 284-307.

Tansley, A.G. 1939. *The British Islands and their Vegetation*. Cambridge University Press, Cambridge.

Tansley, A.G. 1946. *Our Heritage of Wild Nature: A Plea for Organized Nature Conservation*. Cambridge University Press, Cambridge.

Taylor, M., Seago, M., Allard, P. & Dorling, D. 1999. *The Birds of Norfolk*. Pica Press, Robertsbridge.

Taylor, M. 2002. *Guardian Spirit of the East Bank*. Wren Publishing, Sheringham.

Thomas, K. 1984. *Man and the Natural World: Changing Attitudes in England 1500-1800*. Penguin, London.

Thomson, D. 2001. *The People of the Sea*. Canongate Books, Edinburgh.

Thoreau, H.D. 1851. *Walking.* New York, HarperCollins, 1994.

Thoreau, H.D. 1854. *Walden; or, Life in the Woods.* New York: Dover Publications, 1995.

Trett, P. 1978. Scroby Island and its Seals. *Norfolk Bird & Mammal Report* 1978. Norfolk & Norwich Naturalists' Society.

Wallace, D.I.M. 2004. *Beguiled by Birds*. Christopher Helm, London.

Ward, E.M. 1922. *English Coastal Evolution*. Methuen & Co. Ltd., London.

White, D.J.B. 1967. *An Annotated List of the Flowering Plants and Ferns on Blakeney Point, Norfolk*. National Trust, Norfolk.

White, D.J.B. 1969. *An Annotated Checklist of the Birds of Blakeney Point, Norfolk*. National Trust, Norfolk.

White, D.J.B. 1979. The Effects of the Storm of 11 January 1978 on Blakeney Point. *Transactions of the Norfolk & Norwich Naturalists' Society* 25: 267-269.

White, D.J.B. 2005. Blakeney Point and University College London. *The Glaven Historian* 8: 17-20.

White, G. 1789. *The Natural History of Selborne*.

Williamson, H. 1940. *The Story of a Norfolk Farm*. Faber & Faber Ltd., London.

Williamson, K. 1965. *Fair Isle and its Birds*. Oliver & Boyd, Edinburgh and London.

Williamson, T. 2006. *England's Landscape*: *East Anglia*. Collins, London.

Worster, D. 1977. *Nature's Economy*: *The Roots of Ecology*. Sierra Club, San Francisco.

INDEX

Aberdeen University, 109
Africa, 7
Africa, South, 51
Africa, West, 23
Agassiz, Louis, 86
Agriculture Act 1947, 55
Albatross, 27
Alexandria, 47
Alps, The, 142
America, 36, 43, 48, 51
American Forest Service, 53
Anglian glaciation, 86
Anglo-Brabant Massif, 85
Angola, 110
Area of Outstanding Natural Beauty, 59, 138
Argentina, 29
Arnold, E.C., 6, 13-19, 36, 37, 68
Arnold's Marsh, 68
Ashworth, Rev. E.H., 13
Aster, Sea, 41, 42, 137
Atlantic, 54, 115
Auk, 27, 28
Australia, 89
Avocet, 25

Babington, Charles, 44
Badgers, 31
Badger-baiting, 25
Baltic Sea, 108, 125
Baxter, Evelyn Vida, 108
Beacon Hills 82

Bedrock geology, 85
Beetles, 11
Bempton, 27, 28
Benson, Edward Frederic, 146
Beston, Henry, 132
Bioecology, 44
Biome, 44
Biosphere reserve, 59
Biota, 44
Biotic community, 44
Bird-liming, 25
Bird Migration, 113, 116, 118
Bird Observatories Committee, 109
Bird Study, 118
Birmingham, 17
Bishop, Billy, 14
Blackbird, 101
Blair, Hugh, 141
Blake, William, 27
Blakeney, 8, 10, 82-84, 95, 129, 137, 143, 146
Blakeney and Cley Wild Bird Protection Society, 32
Blakeney Channel, 82
Blakeney Freshes, 84
Blakeney Hotel, 36, 143
Blakeney Meals, 44
Bluethroat, 5-8, 10, 15, 16, 23, 36, 104, 107, 108, 111, 112, 115-117
Board of Agriculture, 66
Borrer, Clifford, 13-15, 116
Botany, 2, 39, 43-47, 64

Botanical Society, 12
Bouche d'Erquy, 44
Bramble, 42
Breckland, 142
Brent, William, 13
Breydon Society, 62
Breydon Water, 32, 62
Brightwren, Elizabeth, 28
Bristol Channel, 109
British Association for the Advancement of Science, 12, 106
British Birds, 109
British Ecological Society, 48, 71, 72
British Empire Vegetation Committee, 49
British Ornithologists' Union, 12, 18, 27
British Pathé, 127
British Trust for Ornithology, 109, 113, 118
Britannia, 14, 33
Brittany, 44
Bullfinch, 25
Bunting, Little, 18, 107
Bunting, Ortolan, 112
Bunting, Rustic, 115, 116
Bunting, Snow, 123
Bunting, Yellow-breasted, 17-19
Burg-el-Arab, 47
Burke, Edmund, 141
Bustard, Great, 25
Butterflies, 11, 21

Cairo, 47
Calthorpe, Lord, 64
Cambridge, 27, 44, 48, 88
Cambridgeshire, 63
Campion, Sea, 41
Cant, Michael, 117
Carey, Alfred E., 88
Cart Road, 19
Catlin, George, 60
Catling, M.A., 14
Central Asia, 18, 29
Chance, 33
Channel Islands, 44
Charles II, 83
Chepstow, 17
Chesil Beach, 90
Chiffchaff, 19
Clements, Frederic, 43, 44, 48-54
Cley, 8, 10, 13-17, 33, 35, 68, 81, 83, 95, 96, 110-112, 137, 143
Cley Bird Observatory, 111-113, 115-117
Cley Channel, 9
Climax condition, 44, 50
Coastal geomorphology, 2, 79, 87
Coastal Preservation Committee, 66
Cock-fighting, 26
Coleridge, Samuel Taylor, 26
Collins, Capt. Greenville, 83
Committee for the Survey and Study of British Vegetation, 48
Commons Preservation Society, 61
Concord, Massachusetts, 52
Connops, 13
Connop, Ernest, 17
Conservation Area, 72
Conservation of Seals Act 1970, 128

Constable Country, 142
Cordeaux, John, 106, 107, 116
Couch, Sand, 42
Coues, Elliott, 12
Cowles, Henry Chandler, 43, 48
Cozens-Hardy, A.W., 67
Cranes, 25, 101
Cretaceous period, 85
Cromer, 86, 142, 143
Croydon, 28
Crundall, Alexander, 64
Curlew, 147
Cyclonic approach, 114

Dedham Vale, 142
Deer-hunting, 25
Defoe, Daniel, 145
Descartes, René, 131
Devensian glaciation, 86
Devon, 144
Dock, Curled, 41
Donna Nook, 125
Downs, South, 25
Doyle, Arthur Conan, 143
Dresser, Henry, 17
Drift migration, 114, 118
'Duchess', 14
Duck-decoying, 25
Dunes, 1, 2, 8, 35, 37, 41, 42, 44, 45, 47, 64-67, 79, 80, 82, 84, 90, 92-95, 112, 138, 146, 148
Dungeness, 66, 90
Dunlin, 9
Dunstable Downs, 25
Dust Bowl, 51

Eagle Clarke, William, 107, 108
Eagle, White-tailed, 25
Eales, Bill, 110
Eales, Ted, 110, 126
East Anglia, 1, 87, 89, 90, 142
Eastbourne, 25
Eastbourne College, 13
East Hills, 9
East Prussia, 108
Eastern Daily Press, 18, 35
East Riding Association for the Protection of Sea Birds, 27
Ecosystem, 49
Eddystone Lightship, 107
Edward Grey Institute, 116
Egg-collecting, 24, 25
Eggeling, Joe, 115
Egypt, 71, 102
Elder, 42
Enlightenment, The, 25, 131
Ennion, Eric, 115
Enterprise Neptune, 75
Entomological Society, 12
Epping Forest, 61
Essex, 96, 142
Ethiopia, 102

Faden, William, 84
Faeroe Islands, 94
Fair Isle, 107-109, 112, 115
Farne Islands, 67, 128
Farne Islands Association, 67
Far Point, 82, 84
Fens, The, 142
Ferns, 11
Fieldfare, 101

Fife, 37
First War, 13, 37, 66, 70, 88, 109, 127
Firth of Forth, 108
Fishmongers' Company, 64
Fitter, Richard, 110
Flamborough Head, 27
Flannan Isles, 107
Flatfish, 34, 35
Flowers, 11
Flycatcher, Pied, 113
Flycatcher, Red-breasted, 16, 112
Flycatcher, Spotted, 113
Forestry, 51, 70
Forestry Commission, 62, 67, 70
Fossils, 11
Foxes, 24, 31
Fox-hunting, 25
France, 44
Funnel net, 111
Fur, Fin and Feather Group, 28

Gannet, 28
Gätke, Heinrich, 102, 104-108
Gaze, Reginald, 147
Geese, Brent, 147
Geese, Pink-footed, 115
George Hotel, 67
Germany, 44
Gibraltar Point, 109
Gilpin, William, 140, 142
Glandford, 95
Glaven Ports, 8
Glaven, River, 83, 84, 95, 96
Gledhill, John, 18

Goldcrest, 17, 35, 36, 101, 106, 110, 111
Gorleston, 142
Goshawk, 25
Grass, Marram, 42, 47
Greenland, 115
Gresham's School, 116
Grey, Sir Edward, 29
Grey Seal (Protection) Act 1914, 127
Grouse, Red, 26
Gould, John, 12
Great Coates, 106
Grey, Joanna, 145
Grouse-shooting, 25
Guillemot, 28
Gull, Black-headed, 34
Gull, Herring, 123
Gunn, T.E., 13
Gurney, Quentin, 32

Haeckel, Ernst, 42
Haggard, Lilias Rider, 147
Hair-grass, Grey, 42
Hammond, Charles, 33
Hampstead Heath, 61
Hare, 27, 132
Hare-coursing, 25
Harrier, Marsh, 25, 81
Hartert, Ernst, 18
Harvie-Brown, John, 106
Hebrides, 128, 132, 142
Heligoland, 17, 103, 104, 106-109
Heligoland trap, 108, 111, 116
Heritage Coast, 59, 138
Higgins, Jack, 145

Highlands, 139, 142, 143
Hill, Octavia, 61
Holderness, 90
Holkham, 47
Holkham Meals, 82, 123
Holocene era, 86, 91
Holt, 10, 86, 116
Holt-Cromer ridge, 86
Hood, The, 82, 92, 100, 111, 116
Horned-poppy, Yellow, 41, 137
Horsey, 125
Howell, 19
Hudson, W.H., 29-31
Humber, River, 106
Humboldt, Alexander von, 43
Hunstanton, 143
Hunter, Robert, 61
Huntingdonshire, 63
Hutton, James, 85
Huxley, Julian, 72, 73

Ibis, 12
Ice Age, 86
Iceland, 94, 115
Indiana, 43
Industrial Revolution, 26, 60
International Phytogeographical Expedition, 48
Isostatic rebound, 87
Italy, 142
Ivory Coast, 110

Jamaica, 89
Japanese mist net, 111, 116, 117
Jay, 25
Johnson, Douglas Wilson, 88
Johnson, Dr., 139
Journal of Ecology, 45, 46, 48

Kaliningrad, 108
Kelling, 84
Kent, 8, 66, 96
Kentish Knock lightship, 107
Kestrel, 24
Kinder Scout, 69
Kittiwake, 27, 28
Knot, 9

Laboratory, The, 40, 45, 47, 48, 58, 65
Lack, David, 116, 118
Lake District, 61, 142
Lark, Shore, 107
Lark, Short-toed, 109
Larne, 94
Leopold, Aldo, 53, 54
Leven, Loch, 37
Lichens, 42
Lifeboat House, The, 33, 34, 45, 95
Lilford, Lord, 29
Lincolnshire, 8, 95, 106, 109, 125
Linnaean Society, 12
Linnaeus, Carl, 11, 42
Lithography, 12
Lockley, Ronald, 108
London, 8, 18, 149
Long Hills, The, 82, 92, 93
Long, Sydney, 67, 68
Lopez, Barry, 133
Lorrain, Claude, 140

Lowestoft, 33
Lundy, 109
Lyell, Charles, 85
Lyell, Charles (MP), 127
Lysaght, W.R., 17

Mabey, Richard, 148
Mallard, 30
Manchester, 28
Marrams, The, 82, 92,
Massachusetts, 52
Massingham, H.J., 35
May, Isle of, 108, 109
Mediterranean, 41
Meinertzhagen, Col. R., 109
Midland and Great Northern Railway, 10
Migration Research Officer, 113, 118
Ministry of Agriculture and Fisheries, 127
Ministry of Fisheries, 35
Monk's House, 115
Montaigne, Michel de, 131
Moran, Thomas, 60
Morris, Rev. F., 27
Morston, 10, 19, 75, 82-84, 129, 137, 148
Mortensen, Hans Christian Cornelius, 109
Mosses, 42
Moth, 21
Muir, John, 60
Murre, 28

National Book Award, 133
National Nature Reserve, 56, 72, 73, 75

National Park, 60, 69, 71, 73
National Parks and Access to the Countryside Act 1949, 73
National Trust, 34, 35, 59, 61-69, 71, 72, 75, 111, 128, 137
National Trust Act 1907, 61
Natural Area, 56
Natural England, 138
Nature Conservancy, 73
Nature Reserves Investigation Committee, 70-72
Near Point, 82
Nebraska, 43, 49
Netherlands, The, 96, 114
Newcastle, 7
New Phytologist, 44, 46, 48
Newton, Alfred, 27-29
Norfolk and Norwich Naturalists' Society, 8, 45, 67,
Norfolk Naturalists' Trust, 68
North Channel, 94
North Coates, 116
North Sea, 1, 94, 95, 114, 125
Northern Ireland, 94
Northrepps Hall, 32
Northumberland, 67
Norwich, 67
Norwich School of Artists, 142

'Old Bishop', 14
'Old Bloke', 14
Old Hall Farm, 144
'Old Shuck', 143
Oliver, Francis, Wall, 40, 44-49, 51-55, 63, 64, 68, 71, 88, 89
Ordnance Survey, 84
Orford Ness, 90
Orkney, 108, 128, 132

Osprey, 25
Otters, 31
Otter-hunting, 25
Ousel, Ring, 107, 113
Owl, Short-eared, 24
Oxford, 116
Oystercatcher, 34

Paganini's Restaurant, 18
Parliament, 63
Pashley, Henry Nash, 16-19, 32, 33, 36
Payn, Col. W.A., 13, 36
Pembrokeshire, 108
Pennant, Thomas, 25
Petchora, River, 107
Pheasant, 26
Pheasant-shooting, 25
Phillips, John, 51
Phocine distemper virus, 125
Picturesque, The, 135, 138, 139-143, 149
Pilot House, 18
Pine, Corsican, 47
Pinchen, Robert, 14, 19, 22, 34, 35, 37, 65, 110, 126
Pinchen's Creek, 82
Pinnipedia, 125
Pintail, 30, 37
Pipit, Meadow, 17
Pipit, Richard's, 105, 107, 108, 115
Plantation, The, 37, 47, 58, 113, 116
Pleistocene era, 85
Plover, Grey, 107
Plover, Kentish, 68
Plover, Ringed, 147
Plumage League, 28

Pochard, 30
Polar Sea, 104
Poplar, White, 47
Poppyland, 143
Post-juvenile dispersal, 114
Powell, A.G.P., 147
Power, Fred and George, 7, 8, 10, 13, 14, 16, 104
'Prince', 14, 37
Progressive movement, 51, 54
Puffin, 28
Punt-gunning, 9, 32

Quain Professor, 44, 46

Rabbits, 45, 93
Ragwort, Common, 41, 137
Ramblers' Association, 69
Ramm, Ted, 14-17, 19, 115
Ramsar site, 59
Rats, 24, 31
Rawnsley, Canon Hardwicke, 61
Redshank, 9, 147
Redstart, 15, 36, 113
Redstart, Black, 113
Redwing, 30, 31, 101, 115, 117
Renaissance, 131
Rhine Valley, 142
Richards, Frank, 13, 14
Richardson, Richard, 100, 110, 112, 113, 115-117, 148
Riddington, 146
Riddington Point, 146
Rintoul, Leonora Jeffrey, 108, 109
Riviere, Bernard, 16

Robin, 7, 15, 27, 36, 101, 111, 112
Rockies, 60
Roller, 15
Rollesby Hall, 17
Romantic movement, 26, 29, 60, 141
Rommel, 47
Roosevelt, Theodore, 51
Rossitten, 108, 109
Rothschild, Lord, 18
Rothschild, Nathaniel Charles, 62-64, 66, 69, 76
Rowan, William, 19, 36
Royal Scottish Museum, 107
Royal Society for the Prevention of Cruelty to Animals, 27
Royal Society for the Protection of Birds, 28, 37, 66, 75
Russia, 17, 101, 114
Rybachi, 108

Salisbury, Edward James, 46, 47, 63, 71, 88
Salthouse, 68, 83, 95, 111
Salthouse Broad, 9
Saltmarsh, 1, 2, 30, 41, 42, 44, 47, 66, 72, 75, 79, 82, 83, 90, 93-95, 143, 149
Saltmarsh Coast, 137
Samphire, 41, 42
Sandgrouse, Pallas's, 10, 29
Sandhills, 82, 123
Sandwort, Sea, 41
Saunders, Howard, 13
Saville, Malcolm, 148
Scandinavia, 7, 18, 101, 114

Scientific Area, 73
Scolt Head Island, 67, 89, 92, 110
Scotland, 94
Scott, Clement, 143
Scroby Sands, 126-128
Sea Birds Protection Act 1869, 27
Sea-lavender, Common, 41, 137
Sea Parrot, 28
Sea-purslane, 42
Sea Swallow, 21, 23, 28
Seal, Common, 122, 125-128
Seal, Grey, 122-128, 134
Second War, 52, 69, 109, 147
Sedge, Sand, 42
Seebohm, Henry, 13, 106, 107
Senegal, 110
Sheffield, 106
Shelduck, 9
Sheringham, 90, 143
Shetland, 108, 132
Shingle, 1-5, 7, 8, 41, 42, 44, 46, 47, 64, 66, 67, 72, 79, 81-83, 91-97, 111, 121, 124, 137, 146-149
Shoreline Management Plan, 96
Siberia, 13, 16, 17, 105, 107, 114, 116
Site of Special Scientific Interest, 59, 73, 75, 76
Skokholm, 108
Skylark, 25
Slapton Ley, 90
Snakes, 29
Snipe, Great, 13
Snowdonia, 142

Society for the Prevention of Cruelty to Animals, 26
Society for the Promotion of Nature Reserves, 63, 64, 66, 70, 71, 76
Society for the Protection of Birds, 28, 29
Solan Goose, 28
Southeast Asia, 105
Southern Oceans, 23
Sparrow, House, 25
Sparrowhawk, 25
Spartina, 47
Special Area of Conservation, 59
Special Protection Area, 59
Spence, Barry, 116
Spiders, 29
Spoonbill, 25
Spurn Point, 109, 116
Squirrel, Grey, 52
St. Catharine's College, 88
St. Kilda, 107
Steers, Alfred James, 88-94, 96
Stiffkey, 9, 75, 82, 83, 144, 145, 148
Stint, Little, 107
Stoat, 24
Stonecrop, Biting, 41
Storm surge, 2, 79, 84, 95, 96, 111
Straits of Dover, 87
Stranraer, 94
Streeten, 17
Strong, 19
Sublime, The, 135, 141, 142
Suaeda, 2, 5-7, 35, 41, 46, 95, 101, 111, 117, 123, 148
Succession of vegetation, 41-45, 47, 48, 50, 52, 54, 55, 74,

Suffolk, 96, 142
Sule Skerry, 107
Superficial geology, 86
Surbiton, 64
Surrey, 64
Sussex, 8, 68
Swallow, 23, 101, 102
Systema Naturae, 11

Tamarisk, The, 40, 47
Tansley, Arthur George, 48-55, 57, 58, 63, 69, 71-75
Tarrock, 28
Taxidermist, 10, 16
Taxonomy, 39, 42, 43, 47
Teal, 28, 30
Tern, Arctic, 23, 34
Tern, Common, 10, 23, 24, 34, 35, 37, 110
Tern, Little, 23, 24, 33-35
Tern, Roseate, 32
Tern, Sandwich, 22-24, 34, 35, 37, 110
The Ark, 33
The Geographical Journal, 89
The Times, 28, 30, 65
The Zoologist, 12, 106
Thomson, Arthur Landsborough, 109
Thomson, David, 132
Thoreau, Henry David, 52, 60
Thrift, 41
Thrush, Song, 117
Thrushes, 30
Transactions, 8, 45, 46
Trett, Percy, 18
Tring, 18
Turner, Emma Louise, 110
Turnstone, 16

Twyford Hall, 33

University College, London, 19, 40, 44-48, 64
University, Egyptian, 47
Urals, 105
Ushant, 107

Vermeer, 81

Wakefield, 62
Wallace, Alfred, 13
Walsey Hills, 111
Walton Hall, 62
Warbler, Aquatic, 13, 112
Warbler, Arctic, 19
Warbler, Barred, 8, 112
Warbler, Eversmann's, 19
Warbler, Greenish, 19
Warbler, Icterine, 17, 112
Warbler, Pallas's, 17, 115
Warbler, Radde's, 100, 116
Warbler, Subalpine, 111, 112, 116
Warbler, Willow, 19
Warbler, Yellow-browed, 16, 17, 105, 107, 108, 114-116
Ward, Edith Marjorie, 88
Wardian glass case, 12
Warham, 82
Warming, Eugenius, 43, 48
Wash, The, 81, 126, 128
Watch House, The, 17, 82, 92, 95, 136, 146
Waterton, Charles, 27, 62
Wells, 9, 30, 33, 67, 95

Weybourne, 92
Weybourne Hope, 81, 90
Wheatear, 25, 115
Wheatear, Desert, 18
Whinchat, 113
White, Gilbert, 11, 25, 51, 102
Wicken Fen, 63
Wigeon, 28, 30
Wild Birds Protection Acts, 28
Wild Birds Protection Committee, 37
Wild Birds Protection Society, 33, 37
Wild Fowl Protection Act, 28
Wild Life Conservation Special Committee, 72
Wildfowling, 9, 10, 25, 30, 32, 33, 37
Wildlife Trusts, 76
Williamson, Henry, 110, 144, 145, 147
Williamson, Kenneth, 113-116, 118
Willowherb, Rose-bay, 42
Willughby and Ray, 101
Wisconsin, 53
Wise use philosophy, 51
Witherby, Harry, 109
Wolstonian glaciation, 86
Woodwalton Fen, 63
Wren, St. Kilda, 31
Wryneck, 112
Wye Valley, 142

Yankee Ridge, 82, 93
Yarmouth, Great, 7, 126, 142
Yellowhammer, 17
Yellowstone, 60

Yorkshire, 8, 109
Yorkshire Museum, 35
Youth Hostels Association, 69
Yucatan, 85
Yucca, 47

Zeppelins, 144
Zoological Society, 12